"If you want possibilities, shift your minaset and invest into your personal and professional success, then "A High-Performing Mind" is a must read! This empowering book is full of real-life stories that illustrate and re-enforce incredibly useful insights and strategies that can be applied to your life immediately to manage adversity, build resilience, and experience a more fulfilling life."

Jill Hewlett, Brain Fitness Expert
Author: Common Sense Uncommonly Practiced

"The lessons Andrew has shared have helped me navigate challenges in athletics, academics, and life in general. Andrew is an outstanding coach, who is without comparison in his understanding of how to build mental strength and a resilient mind. He helped me believe that anyone could succeed on any given day in sports or otherwise. Additionally, Andrew helped me develop the tools to recover from challenges and setbacks and realize my potential. I would highly recommend A High-Performing Mind to anyone looking to excel or to build resilience to navigate life's challenges."

Dr. Alexi Gosset, MD
Harvard Squash Team, 2019 National Champions

"A High Performing Mind is an amazing book!!!! Everything flows so well both in the writing and the logic. It's very light and approachable, easy to read, but weaves in important points seamlessly. I felt really inspired just reading it."—**J.K.**

"I finished your wonderful and insightful book last week and want to tell you that it was a 'learning experience' for me and reminded me of the true value of focus back in the days when I was running marathons. Congratulations on your 'work of art'. I have ordered 5 copies of your book on Amazon - one for each of my sons! More people need to read this. You are a wonderful writer and certainly have a way of getting your message across."

—N.P.

"When taking the time to work with a coach, there are a range of best practices that make a significant difference in getting results that last. Andrew knows coaching methods and processes that bring out the best performance from those he works with."

Jacoline Loewen, MBA, ICD.D
Author: Money Magnet: Attracting Investors to your Business

"You will laugh as you're taken through some of the most valuable knowledge in the world…worth many thousands of dollars. This book will likely be the best investment you've ever made. Andrew was the key to my sports success at the World Junior Championships and Division 1 NCAA level."

Julien Gosset, Former Canadian #1 Junior Squash Player
Two time NCAA National Champion with Harvard University.

"A High-Performing Mind stands out for its authenticity and relatability. Thompson shares his own journey with vulnerability, making it clear that the path to high performance is not linear but is accessible to anyone willing to commit to personal growth. The book serves as a powerful reminder that with the right mindset, strategies, and dedication, living your best life is within your grasp."
—A.N.

"I loved this book. It's clear, easy to read, and implementable. It's filled with simple yet profound concepts, that when actioned, lead to obvious performance and life enhancements. A highly recommended read."
—C.Z.

"A High Performing Mind is a really great resource for anyone who is looking for actionable ways to meet their goals. For me, the most helpful parts of AHPM are when Andrew describes how to overcome the common ways that we self-sabotage on the path to success. I've read quite a few business and self-help books and AHPM sets itself apart because its guidance is easy to understand and apply in your own life."
—S.W.

A HIGH-PERFORMING MIND

STRENGTHEN YOUR MIND AND LIVE YOUR BEST LIFE

ANDREW D. THOMPSON

ISBN 978-1-7390210-6-1

*This book is dedicated to
My father for teaching me to always
do my best and to my mother for
being a constant source of love,
support, and wisdom. To my wife Katie
for her continued love & patience and my
two beautiful children.*

CONTENTS

INTRODUCTION: From Weakness to Strength 11

PART I
– THE FOUNDATION –
STRENGTHENING THE HEART

CHAPTER 1: Desire, Dirty Discipline, and
Warrior Mentality - Empowering the Will 33

CHAPTER 2: Did Someone Say It Was Supposed To Be Easy?
Building Resilience and Overcoming Adversity 49

CHAPTER 3: Always Do Your Best -
Even If the Fish Dies 68

CHAPTER 4: Openness and Self-Honesty -
Accelerating Personal Growth and Improvement 82

CHAPTER 5: Sticks and Stones May Break My Bones -
But Painful Words Can Strengthen Me 92

PART II
– THE MAIN FLOOR –
STRENGTHENING THE MIND

CHAPTER 6: What Else Do You Really Want?
Creating Your Master Plan 109

CHAPTER 7: Explore, Experiment, and Fail Your Way to
Excellence - Learning from Our Setbacks and Failures 125

CHAPTER 8: The Process Not the Outcome - Afterburners
and the Power of Patience 141

CHAPTER 9: Getting Unstuck - Finding the Positives
in the Negatives... 153

CHAPTER 10: Say YES to Fear - And Keep Going! 168

CHAPTER 11: Performing at Our Best -
Using Present Moment Focus To Access "Flow" 183

CHAPTER 12: Finding the Courage -
Following Your Heart, Taking Chances, and Seizing
Opportunities 211

PART III

– THE VERANDA –

STRENGTHENING THE SPIRIT

CONCLUSION: The End is Just the Beginning
of Your New Future.. 223

Contact 228

About the Author 229

INTRODUCTION

From Weakness to Strength

My eyes sprung open. The room was pitch dark. Something wasn't right.

I glanced at the clock on the nightstand; it was 2AM. It took me a minute to get my bearings and remember I was at a mediocre hotel, not far from where I would be coaching a bunch of junior athletes at a national tournament the following day. But more importantly, something definitely didn't feel normal. I had this strange vibrating sensation in my chest, and I felt unusually weak—I could barely lift my arms and legs. A wave of fear gripped the pit of my stomach.

I slowly sat up in bed and immediately decided to abandon the three-day fast I'd started just a day and a half earlier. I had fasted a handful of times over the years—simply because I felt it was healthy for the body—and I had coordinated this fast to coincide with my drive to the tournament. I had only done 36-hour fasts in the past, but this time decided to go for it and see if I could make it a full three days. Clearly, life had other plans.

My mind fixated on the feeling that I should eat something as soon as possible. I crawled out of bed and looked around the room, only finding a bag of almonds and some water. I grabbed a handful and started chewing away, but it was quickly obvious the almonds weren't going to cut it.

Feeling lightheaded with a pounding headache and still profoundly weak, I got dressed, which was a colossal effort. I headed outside to find more to eat and spotted a fast-food restaurant across the parking lot, thankfully, it was open 24 hours.

I sat down at a table, my head spinning. The dining room seemed somehow darker than it should have been, and it was hard to focus. *What is going on?!* I sat down at a table and waited for what felt like an eternity for my egg and cheese sandwich, all while wondering when I would feel better.

The sandwich did little to help, so I headed back across the parking lot to my room, hoping I could sleep it off.

When I woke up a few hours later, it was finally light out, but I still felt terrible. An innate sense that I needed to eat something gnawed at me again, but I couldn't figure out what. I eventually decided some orange juice might do the trick. *Maybe my blood sugar is low or something?*

I got into my car, still feeling awful, and drove in a random direction. I found a local convenience store nearby, stumbled in, and bought some juice and a couple of other snacks hoping this would reset my energy levels. But when I returned to the car and drank the juice, nothing changed. I still felt weak and completely out of it. Now I was seriously concerned. As I got in the car and started back toward the hotel, I didn't get far before that vibrating sensation returned with a vengeance. This time, though, I started to feel it throughout my arms, and my fingers began to cramp and uncontrollably curl into fists. I could barely open my hands. Panic rolled in like a wave hitting my chest; *what the hell is happening to me?*

Any vestige of denial that something was seriously wrong evaporated, I needed help and I needed it immediately. I managed to pull over, but by now I was having immense trouble concentrating. Hunched over with my head pressed against the steering wheel, I dialed 911.

They arrived quickly, put me on a stretcher, and took me to the local hospital, just a few minutes away. In the hallway waiting area, I lay curled into a ball on a gurney, lightheaded and unsure if I would lose consciousness. My breathing was labored, and I felt like I couldn't get enough air—I had no idea why.

The doctors didn't seem to be any more clued in than I was to what was going on. They ran a bunch of tests, including some blood work, while I lay there in intense distress. I couldn't believe how weak I felt.

After a few hours alone, focused on my breathing, and willing myself through this unexpected nightmare, the doctor returned with a report: one of my blood markers—phosphate—came back unusually low. While they couldn't figure out why, they placed a phosphorus drip into my vein to bring me back to normal levels as quickly as possible.

After monitoring me for the next 12 hours to ensure I was stable, I was finally released. Given no history of anything similar, the doctors and I chalked it up to the fasting. They were quick to tell me that starving myself for 36 hours was a terrible idea and not to do anything like that again. I didn't need any convincing and silently vowed my fasting days were over!

The next day, I woke up relieved to feel more or less normal. I spent the day coaching and figured the doctors were right, the fast was to blame and the situation was behind me. I hit the road at the end of the day and made the three-hour drive back home. I assumed the whole thing was a bizarre one-off incident. But I was wrong. What I experienced was just the beginning of the worst year and a half of my life.

The next day, I woke up and went to work as I would have on any regular Monday morning.

Within an hour or two though, after walking up a flight of stairs, I started to feel incredibly weak again, only this time, the symptoms I'd experienced before were even worse.

My heartbeat was weak, and the intense vibrating was back in my arms and chest, spreading up into my face this time. My hands began curling uncontrollably inward again, and the world darkened and receded. Again, I struggled to breathe normally, and my co-worker, who could see that something was catastrophically wrong, asked me what he should do. I told him to call an ambulance.

It was ten terrifying minutes before they arrived, and it felt like an eternity. Again, they took my vitals and again I was strapped onto a stretcher and taken to the hospital.

By the time I was finally seen, I could barely gather my thoughts. My speech was slurred as I did my best to relay the events from the last couple of days. They ran similar blood tests, which came back with an alarmingly low phosphate level of .19 mmol/L. It was a life-threatening drop the doctor said he'd never seen before in his ten years of working in the emergency department.

Fortunately, they started taking things a lot more seriously from then on, and I was quickly administered another phosphorus IV. When my breathing finally evened out and the sense of imminent danger had begun to fade, I learned that the low phosphate levels put me at risk of sudden heart and respiratory failure.

Worst-case scenarios raced through my mind. I worried this was the end for me and I'd never see my family again

The doctors admitted me to the Intensive Care Unit to monitor me more closely. I called my wife to tell her what was going on. Despite phosphate pills and the IV drip, I still had numerous episodes of life-threateningly low phosphate levels.

It turns out that phosphate is one of the most essential elements in our bodies. It controls all energy production, and when it gets low, vital organs like our kidneys, heart, brain, and lungs start to shut down.

The next few days in the ICU were an emotional roller coaster ride. I was so weak most of the time I couldn't stand without assistance. My family took shifts, staying with me to help me through my days. I had repeated waves of breathing difficulties, and I remember lying there willing and praying my heart would keep beating. I was put through a battery of tests, but nobody seemed to know what was going on or, more importantly, *why.*

I was confused and afraid. How could this be happening? Just a few days before, I had been doing 400-meter sprints at the track, and now this! Even though I was in my early forties at the time, I was still in extremely good shape. I regularly exercised one to two hours a day—a long-standing habit from my younger years as a professional athlete. My mind couldn't comprehend how I could go from that to feeling like I might die at any moment in such a short span of time.

I oscillated between feeling like I was at death's door and being sure I'd wake up the next day feeling completely normal. As far as I was concerned, this whole thing shouldn't be happening.

After about four days in the ICU, armed with pills and containers for tests, I was sent home.

Rather than being a relief, getting back home was a massive reality check that painted a picture of a bleak future. I had to crawl up the stairs to reach my bedroom because I was so weak. When I finally made it to the top of the stairs, I lay there panting. It took over 20 minutes to catch my breath from the effort as if I had just run a series of 100-meter sprints.

Despite all this, my denial held firm. I was sure my recovery would just be a matter of time. But this couldn't have been further from the truth.

I spent the next four and a half months lying in bed upwards of 22 hours a day. I remember being so weak that I couldn't handle someone raising their voice at me or having an intense conversation without needing to lie down for a few hours to recover. I also remember feeling so terrible that I couldn't make it downstairs to celebrate my son's third birthday. It was devastating to miss something so important.

Over those first few months, depression set in hard, and I wallowed in the fear that I'd never recover. I cried almost daily over everything I'd lost; afraid I would never be physically active again or be able to support my family financially. I felt imprisoned in the shell of a body that was incapable of functioning normally.

I saw a dozen different specialists and heard as many theories, but none seemed to definitively explain why my body wouldn't absorb phosphate properly anymore. I eventually gave up on the medical system and decided I'd have to find my own way out of this health crisis. I began reading everything I could on low phosphate conditions, including the latest scientific research papers.

On top of this, I also started monitoring my diet and looking for patterns across days when I felt better or worse. Slowly, over many months of intense scrutiny and documenting everything I ate, I started to develop an eating protocol to manage my condition.

During this time, I drew heavily on my many years of competing in sports. Through sheer determination, I was able to return to work for one to two hours a day after about four and a half months of being mostly bedridden. I slowly built on this as I gained more insight into what food choices helped and which caused me problems. Two hours a day eventually turned into three, then four, and so on. I was very fortunate to have a place of work that was so supportive to me during this challenging time.

By the year and a half mark, I was back to regular eight-hour days; however, I still had to contend with alarming and random drops in my phosphate levels, occasional seizures, and routine trips to the ER. My phosphate lows became so familiar to me that I could accurately predict what my blood levels would be before my results came back from the lab.

The doctors still had no solutions, but over the next three years, I found more ways to manage my condition through my diet.

I still had terrifying energy lows, but I identified certain foods that were rich in phosphate, which helped me stay more stable.

I wouldn't be able to exercise or exert myself much beyond a resting heart rate without severe symptoms for another five years, but thankfully I could work again and support and care for my wife and kids.

While I wouldn't have wished anything like this on my worst enemy, having a life-altering health experience did have its positives—even if they weren't apparent for a long time.

Before this experience, I'd never have thought of myself as mentally weak—and I don't think anyone else would have either given the self-discipline and determination I'd always found to achieve my goals, but managing through a life-threatening health condition, made me a better, stronger, and more capable human being.

Over time, I developed more resilience and discovered new levels of personal discipline I didn't know I possessed. I became more adept at managing the emotional lows from my now regular setbacks. I learned to do my best, even when I was far from feeling optimal. I became more resourceful because I was forced to continuously find ways to adapt.

The extremely strict diet I used to maintain my energy levels radically improved my health over those first few years. It included no sugar consumption (because of the inflammatory effect), other low-inflammatory considerations, and eating what might be considered dinner for breakfast and something light for dinner. I had more energy this way.

I also no longer drank alcohol, and everything I ate had to be plain to avoid unexpected reactions from unknown ingredients in seasonings and sauces. I learned to sleep propped upwards to help my organs metabolize nutrients; otherwise, my body wouldn't get the phosphate it needed, and I'd feel awful the next day. It turns out that gravity plays a big role in making it easier to break down food into the required elements.

For the longest time, watching TV or playing video games made me feel terrible. It's hard to appreciate when you feel normal, but these things elicit emotional reactions, stress, and body tension that impact our energy levels. When you are as weak as I was, this type of emotional exertion could leave me feeling exhausted for hours.

I became incredibly attuned to my body because it was so sensitive and reactive to everything. This vigilance was required for many years, but all of it contributed to reestablishing a relatively normal life as my body slowly started to function more efficiently.

My expectations of how good life should be and what I should be able to do were completely reset. I went from feeling it was my right, in a sense, to have the ability to be physically active and exercise to simply being grateful for being alive, making it through a day without debilitating symptoms, and being able to put in a full day of work and support my family.

Even though my next five years were punctuated with life-threatening energy lows, hospital stays, intense bouts of chest and kidney pain, mental fog, difficulty concentrating, burning sensations throughout my body, frequently feeling like I might pass out, and often feeling like I couldn't take in enough oxygen, over time I started to develop a quiet confidence that I could handle pretty much anything that came my way.

If it hadn't been for the healing diet I carefully developed over the years—designed to optimize energy production and cleanse my body of toxins—I might still be bedridden. I have become a big believer in Hippocrates' famous words: "Let food be thy medicine and medicine be thy food."

From the time I was a teenager, I had been obsessed with always performing at my best and finding mental approaches to excel in my life. Yet here I was, far from high performing, but determined to recover and relying on the many life lessons I'd learned in my sporting and coaching days to get me through the most challenging period of my life.

My health crisis made it clear that life is rarely easy, and there's usually no straight line to success. It can throw unexpected challenges at us and we might lack the skills and know-how needed to succeed and have to find new ones. There can be a host of obstacles that can stop us in our tracks, like negative thinking, self-sabotage, hurtful words from others, fears, setbacks, failures, and the occasional disaster to just name a few.

I came to see that getting through a prolonged health crisis wasn't much different from what I learned and lived as a high-performance coach and athlete. Life wasn't cooperating with my plans and had hit me hard. I was confronted with a bunch of unexpected hurdles that I had to overcome to continue living the life I imagined. Similar to when I wanted to excel in sports, I had to develop the skills and know-how I needed to reach my goals, only this time my goal was recovery.

It was easy to get caught up in my fear and feel discouraged from all the setbacks and failures I endured—and I did get caught up in them repeatedly. Negative thoughts and emotions haunted me daily. I struggled to see how I would ever be able to extricate myself from the quagmire I found myself drowning in. I was determined, though, to eventually recover and not let the illness define or convince me that there wouldn't be some light at the end of the tunnel.

I knew that there were steps anyone could take to not react negatively or self-destructively in the face of challenging circumstances. I understood how to do this in sport, but I had to learn to do this in every area of my life, including in this very personal aspect of my health.

It took years. I failed often along the way, but fortunately, made it to a better place in the end. Whatever your goal, even if you're facing overwhelming odds, it's my hope the insights, lessons, and mental tools in *A High-Performing Mind* will help you through as well.

The Problem

The world we live in today is full of impressive technological advances aimed at enhancing our lives in a multitude of ways and allowing us to enjoy a variety of modern-day conveniences. There have been extraordinary leaps in many areas of society, including medical advances, which have contributed to eradicating many diseases and extending the human life span. There are others, though, that we may enjoy immensely but also come with unintended consequences that negatively impact our strength of our mind, emotional resilience, and our ability to work productively toward improving our lives.

It's no secret that social media robs us of our free time because it's so compelling to our brains and has been shown to lower self-esteem and create unrealistic perceptions of other people's success and happiness. Inventions like AI, the Internet, and GPS are remarkable. They bring nearly the sum total of human knowledge to our fingertips, providing nearly any answer and can do our work for us. But they also reduce our capacity to figure things out for ourselves, our ability to remember details, and atrophy our independent, creative, and critical thinking skills.

I can think of countless times when I elected to spend excessive hours watching TV, browsing the web, or getting lost in social media instead of choosing something that would improve my life experience. There's nothing wrong with these things of course, but it's all about moderation. Exercising, working on a hobby, passion, or skill, going for a walk to think and clear my head, spending time with someone I cared about, or putting more time into finding ways to make some extra money are all choices, amongst others, that would have been life-enhancing instead of depleting when taken to excess.

The world has become far easier for us physically as well, we often don't have to walk as much or climb stairs, and so much of our work is now automated. These things have their undeniable benefits, but unfortunately also lead to the decline of our physical health and well-being.

There are even subtler impacts on our strength of mind from our devices, which eliminate our need to wait, endure the discomfort of boredom, and occupies our attention to the point where we ignore loved ones and opportunities to do meaningful things. This leads to the desire for instant gratification, which erodes our personal will and self-discipline and increases our preference to choose ease and entertainment over activities and pursuits that truly enhance the quality of our lives.

Technology represents incredible advancements in elements of the evolution of human society. At the same time however, there is a profound cost to the strength of our minds and the happiness of our hearts and spirits —if we're not vigilant and careful.

A High-Performing Mind is about finding this balance and reclaiming our inner strength, resilience, and personal power.

How This Book Can Help

I wrote *A High-Performing Mind* to empower and help you to exercise and increase your mental strength, emotional balance and resilience, and to expand your ability and understanding of how to overcome any challenge or setback, make meaningful improvements in your life, and achieve your goals. It is intended to help you excel and live your optimal life, no matter your circumstances.

My goal is to share the insights, lessons, and mindsets I've learned over my lifetime as an athlete, high-performance coach, executive in the hospitality industry, and fellow human being who has had to battle through some intensely challenging times.

My experiences have helped me understand that it's possible to find our best responses during our most difficult times and, as a result, to achieve better experiences in the areas of our lives that matter most to us. When we have the right mindset, no matter the external circumstances, we can improve how we feel and keep ourselves focused on the outcomes we're striving for so we can thrive in our lives.

If you've ever had something important not work out the way you hoped, failed to reach a goal, performed below your expectations, struggled with your health or relationships, been stopped by fear, blocked by nerves, pulled down by negativity, or sidelined by unexpected, life-altering setbacks, then you're in the right place.

In the chapters ahead, we'll progress through a series of simple steps to give you the mental tools, life-changing habits, and mindsets needed to expand your capabilities. These steps are designed to help you develop your inner strength and understanding of what it takes to access your best and find your resilience and emotional balance when it matters most.

How It All Started

My first lesson on how to succeed came from my dad whose main message when I was a kid was to always work hard. Thanks to this lesson, my natural desire to excel, and a willingness to put in whatever time and effort was necessary to get the results I was looking for, I had some initial successes.

While my dad's advice helped me to a point, I still struggled with setbacks, failures, and an inability to achieve certain outcomes I wanted. It became clear that hard work wasn't the whole equation. I needed something more to consistently perform at my best and find the success I wanted.

I became passionate about finding ways to excel. I also wanted to get to the root of what was holding me back. When I started coaching, I found the same obstacles that held me back also kept my athletes from achieving the success they wanted. I wanted to know what people who excelled in their lives did to consistently get the most out of themselves. What did they do differently than everyone else?

This line of questioning led to my fascination with peak performance. I wanted to achieve my goals and help others do the same. So, I read every book, article, and scientific study I could get my hands on about the science of change, personal transformation, and peak performance.

This research expanded beyond sports into any pursuit where I noticed someone accomplishing extraordinary things. I wanted to understand how the minds of high-performing people worked and how they adapted their particular circumstances to achieve success. What were their thought processes? How did they navigate through their fears, failures, and moments of doubt? How were they able to find positive responses to adversity and change themselves—and sometimes even the world around them—in profoundly beneficial ways?

Through this lifelong dedication to achieving excellence in my own pursuits, research, experimentation, and working with high performers in sports, business, and life in general, I came to identify the most common characteristics they all shared. This process also led to discovering the most effective mental tools, mindsets, and approaches people could use to face their doubts and fears, overcome adversity, and expand their capabilities so they could achieve their goals and live their most fulfilling lives.

In addition to the above, going through my own personal and health related challenges, I came to see that many of these insights, mindsets, and approaches could also be applied to areas outside of sports and business. When I started applying these mental tools in my own life, my interactions with others gradually improved. I became less insecure and more confident, and I spent more time finding creative solutions rather than fixating on whatever problems I was facing. I felt more emotionally resilient and spent less time feeling unhappy and stuck in negative thinking patterns. In addition, I started to consistently access my best more often and enjoyed better results in my pursuits.

It became clear to me that what holds us back from getting the most out of ourselves, in any area of our lives, is our minds.

The principles we'll explore in *A High-Performing Mind* can be applied to anything we experience and wish to improve—from sports, to business, to our health and personal lives. We'll find out how to strengthen our minds, build our resilience, and be at our best, which we'll need to get through life's biggest challenges, achieve our goals, and live our optimal lives.

What to Expect

As the title suggests, the phrase "high performing" is used often throughout the following pages, but what does it truly mean?

At its core, it's about tapping into our inner strength to achieve the best results possible from ourselves in the areas of our lives that matter most. Despite being unable to control what happens to us, we can still develop the ability to make the most out of every situation.

As you integrate the lessons and mental tools in A High-Performing Mind, with a little time and effort, you will notice yourself living a more fulfilling life.

Each chapter in this book can be thought of as part of a path up a nearby hill. At the top, you'll achieve a high-performing mind that is strong and capable of making your life better instead of inadvertently worse.

We start off at the base, each section gradually taking you higher and providing the mental tools necessary to reach the next milestone along the way. I suggest reading the chapters in order and becoming familiar with the lessons and mental approaches offered in each by practicing and using them before moving on.

There's no need to rush. Take breaks as needed and make sure to integrate the new lessons and tools as you progress into the next segment of the climb.

One of the core lessons in *A High-Performing Mind* is that anything worthwhile usually takes time and effort to achieve, and there will likely be challenging moments along the way. Reading this book will be no different. You will encounter ideas and concepts that will take time and repetition to understand, integrate, and apply. Those who persevere will make it to the top of the hill and benefit the most.

A High-Performing Mind will also challenge your critical thinking skills. While nearly every lesson and tool in the pages ahead is supported by a wealth of scientific research and the latest innovations in peak performance and psychology, they are also founded in common sense thinking. It's my hope that you will vet these tools, habits, and mental approaches personally, and determine if they work for you or not.

People tend to decide if something is valid based on who has suggested it before considering the quality and accuracy of the information being delivered. I suggest switching this around as you read *A High-Performing Mind*. Take in the information, consider if it has value, try it out and see if it works for you. Keep it if it does. Throw it aside if it doesn't.

Every story in *A High-Performing Mind* is true. The only deviation from this is in the occasional line or two of dialogue that I didn't recall exactly or in an attempt to inject a little flow or humor.

I have also changed the names and identifiers of the people referenced in the stories ahead to protect their privacy. The stories, however, are etched in my memory the way I have related them.

It's my sincere hope that you'll find something of value in the pages ahead that help you on your journey to a better life experience. At minimum, you'll find an honest account of a lifetime of coaching and exploration of the mind, aimed at helping people find their best in any situation.

The first step of our journey naturally begins in the first section of the book "Building the Foundation." We're not going to get far without a few important tools like determination, a little discipline, some mental strength and resilience, an empowering attitude and willingness to try our best, open-mindedness to improve a little bit each day, a willing heart, and a positive perspective.

We'll start building some of these right away in Chapter 1, which will begin by introducing you to two very important and powerful mental tools that you will already be familiar with but may not use in an optimal way. They are meant to inspire you and ensure your success on your journey by strengthening your mind and your will to succeed.

Get ready to harness the power of your desire, then we'll find out exactly what "Dirty Discipline" is and how it can improve your life.

Let's get started!

PART I

— THE FOUNDATION —

STRENGTHENING THE HEART

CHAPTER 1

Desire, Dirty Discipline, and Warrior Mentality

Empowering the Will

Desire can make us accomplish extraordinary things. I have observed people, who seemingly without the know-how or required skill, spontaneously improvise in unexpected ways to achieve remarkable results—all born out of an intense determination to succeed.

Desire is a high-octane fuel for our bodies that can turbocharge our energy and enable us to completely immerse ourselves in anything we are focused on. Desire brings many great benefits, including passion, the ability to work daily toward an important goal, concentration, energy, and engagement, to name a few.

It also comes in varying degrees of intensity, depending on what we have our sights set on. When our desire is high, it can move us with great speed and intensity towards the outcomes we are aiming for.

Without genuine desire, we aren't going to get very far in achieving our goals. On the other hand, when we follow our heart's desires, the world seems to fall into alignment with us, and awe-inspiring things can happen in our lives.

When I graduated from university, I landed a job in a pharmaceutical marketing research firm in Montreal. Admittedly, I wasn't particularly excited about it, but I needed to work; I had student debts to pay.

Truth be told, in the back of my mind, all I wanted to do was play squash, a sport I loved and competed in on my school's varsity team.

Anytime I considered my circumstances, my lack of enthusiasm for my marketing job was obvious, but intellectually I saw it as the responsible choice—something I should do. At the same time, however, my heart had other opinions. Every time I thought about playing squash, I got super excited, and my heart clearly and wholeheartedly agreed with this idea. I swear I could practically hear it shouting "squash, squash, squash," with every beat. It probably helped that I have a good imagination.

When I was honest about what I truly desired, playing squash was the answer. All I wanted to do was train and play in every free moment I had—I couldn't get enough of it. I had an intense yearning to keep improving so that one day I would be good enough to play on the professional world tour.

There was just one big problem with my plan. I may have done well at the varsity level, but I was nowhere near good enough to play on the world tour and make enough money to support myself or the significant travel expenses this plan would entail.

Part of the equation I also had to consider was the unfortunate fact that squash was a low-profile sport in the grand scheme of things—there wasn't much money in the game. This was particularly the case for anyone outside the top 50 or so players in the world, which definitely wasn't going to be where I started. Given all this, I had no idea how I would make my heart's unrealistic, ill-advised dream, a reality.

This was the state of affairs until about a week before I was supposed to start my new pharmaceutical marketing gig.

I was playing squash one day with a pro friend of mine named Joe. Once we finished up, we sat around stretching and chatting and Joe casually mentioned that they were looking for a squash teaching professional at a local racket club, not too far from where I lived. He asked if the position was something I'd be interested in.

I initially scoffed at the idea. "Teaching pro? That's ridiculous; I could never do that."

My heart wasn't buying this answer though, and the idea stuck in my mind like a splinter. *I just can't see myself being a teaching pro,* I'd say to myself. My heart wanted nothing of it; "squash, squash, squash" was again its reply. But I eventually caved. My curiosity was piqued, and I wanted to hear more about this opportunity.

A couple of days later, after a phone call with Joe, I found myself at a large and prominent tennis and squash facility, seated across a large desk from the club manager interviewing for the position.

I'll never forget that interview. It lasted about two hours, and at the end of it, given that nobody else had applied, I was offered the job. I would be working about 20-25 hours a week, which included teaching a bunch of lessons to club members who wanted to improve their games. This would leave me plenty of daily training time to get my game up to world tour tournament levels. It was the perfect solution, and ironically, it paid better than that marketing job I was holding onto so tightly.

I left the interview ecstatic. I couldn't believe my luck and more importantly, I couldn't wait to start!

I had followed my heart's desire and things were working out in unexpected ways. This path eventually led to a move to Toronto, where I landed a fantastic job and over time, worked my way up the ranks into a senior leadership position in a very successful organization.

More importantly, I met my would-be wife not long afterward. Fast forward several years, and we have two amazing kids and a wonderful life together in a fantastic community. I could never have predicted that a simple, single decision to take a job could lead to all this. And it all began with desire.

Tool #1: Desire

As you embark into the pages ahead, you will also need to be clear about what you really want. What does your heart tell you?

Let's perform a quick check right now and find out. Are you clear about what you truly desire? Do you have a primary goal in mind? Pick one thing right here and now to focus on and write it down. Once you've done that, put it somewhere you can't miss so that you'll see it every day. Can you feel your desire for that one thing right now in your gut or heart when you think about it? If not, pick something else you want to achieve and care about until you're sure.

Consciously acknowledging this goal will lock it in. If you get excited and can feel it somewhere in your body when you think about it, you've successfully used the power of your desire; the first tool in this chapter.

You've now completed your first step up the hill to a high-performing mind, which gives you a little more mental strength than you had before. Being aligned with your desires makes you stronger and more unified in your mind and actions.

Step two? Let's make sure that you're also armed with enough discipline to follow through on that desire.

Tool #2: Dirty Discipline

Now that you've harnessed the power of your personal will, you've already started strengthening your mind. This second tool will help with any tendencies to procrastinate and enable you to start taking the steps you'll need to improve your capabilities and begin creating the foundation to achieve your primary goal.

I like to refer to this next tool as "Dirty Discipline." To be fair, the word discipline, by itself, doesn't have the best reputation. It's often associated with pain and punishment, which sounds the opposite of fun, but there's no denying its usefulness. Admittedly, it can be easy for some to adopt, but not so much for others. The good news, though, is that any amount of discipline above and beyond what you currently have will be an improvement and serve you in powerful and helpful ways.

But let's back up. Discipline in this context simply refers to doing something on a regular basis. No punishment required! Discipline is also much easier to find when it's supported by having intense passion for whatever it is that you're pursuing. In this case, you rarely need to think about discipline because the daily habit takes care of itself—you just can't wait to do it.

At other times, however, it can be challenging to focus, particularly when you haven't strengthened your mind enough yet or established the habit of doing something on a regular basis. This is where "Dirty Discipline," comes in, because it will improve your ability to build a regular habit to make changes in your life in exciting new ways.

So, what's the "dirty" part in "Dirty Discipline?" It simply refers to the concept of giving yourself a little latitude in creating the habit of doing something on a regular basis to move you closer to achieving your goals.

Using the "dirty" approach to discipline is a great starting point. It means you recognize and acknowledge that you will be clear about what you want. However, you will likely have good days and less productive days when building and sustaining a somewhat regular habit of putting in time and effort toward achieving your goals. Of course, we all wish we had the self-discipline that some people exhibit—where they decide what they want to achieve, set their mind to it, and then take daily actions to make it happen. This is ideal, but for most of us, achieving our goals is a lot "dirtier," and there's nothing wrong with that. It might just take a little longer.

Using the "dirty" approach, means it may take you a bit of time to get going, you may get knocked off track for a few days before stopping entirely for a while, but then you pick up again where you left off.

Every time you pick back up, you try to do a little more, go a little longer, and slowly build up your discipline muscle until you are stringing several uninterrupted days in a row together. So, It may not be as clean or fast a process as doing it daily without missing, but you will still get there and constantly improve along the way.

If you already have the discipline to do something regularly, you are on your way. You just have to decide what you want to achieve, set your mind to it, and then specifically plan your daily actions to make it happen. We'll dive a little deeper into this in chapter 6.

If ever you get discouraged about your progress or ability to be consistent, remember, "Dirty Discipline" is a very good starting point and without a doubt, far better than having no discipline…

Tool #3: Empower Your Personal Will- One Small Step at a Time

As I described in the introduction, I was in good shape throughout my life due to my passion to excel in the sports I played. This abruptly ended in 2016, when I was first stricken with the phosphate related illness, which left me bedridden for months. It was the beginning of a long and slow decline in my physical health and, obviously, any semblance of fitness.

This, unfortunately, lasted a long time. Although I attempted to gently exercise on numerous occasions in those first few years, the resulting debilitating symptoms meant that I had to give up exercise completely for several years.

Finally, around the beginning of 2022, my body seemed to have recovered to the point where I could exercise gently again and not notice any symptoms unless I overdid it. If, on a given day, I did push myself too hard, I would feel terrible, but it would pass in a few hours. This was a huge improvement over the past, where I would have been bedridden for days due to similar levels of effort. It became apparent that I was making progress and could tolerate exercise better than at any point in the previous six years. My return to some semblance of regular exercise marked a significant milestone in my journey to recovery.

I have to admit that even as someone who previously trained over four hours a day, it was shocking how challenging it was to build a regular exercise routine from scratch. My body had become very accustomed to not exerting itself, and it was difficult to break past this physical and mental barrier.

Determined to get back into some form of good shape, with modest goals to lose a few pounds around my midsection and be able to keep up with my wife and kids on nature hikes, I decided to begin with weight-lifting because, at that point, I was still quite nervous to inadvertently over-exert myself with cardiovascular exercise like biking. The consequences of overdoing it with cardiovascular exercise were still quite terrifying at that point, so weights it was.

As mentioned, it was hard to get past the complacency I had built over the previous five years as I recovered from my illness. I began by resolving to lift weights three times per week and started small, choosing weights about a quarter of what I would have done in the past. For example, if it was a bicep curl, I started with a 10lb dumbbell and only did one set in those early weeks. I slowly built from there. Two exercises my first time became four after the first two weeks, then five, and six after two months, and so on. I continued this until I reached about ten exercises for each workout, which took a few months.

The bottom line? I started very small in every aspect to ensure I would and could do it. I committed to those three times a week, and on days I didn't feel like doing much, I still did something, even if my workout lasted only a few minutes and consisted of one exercise. I chose to "touch it" regularly, even for a minute or two, to honor the habit instead of skipping a session.

It was about building up the habit of working out again and making sure I made it easy to repeat my three times a week until I got to the point where the habit sustained itself, and it felt easy to get my workouts in. Since then, I have reduced the weights but can now do forty-five-minute cardio sessions three times per week, something I couldn't have imagined just a few years ago. I'm happy to report, I can keep up with my wife and kids on hikes again.

Prioritizing Long-Term Gain Over Short-Term Pain and Discomfort

It can be challenging to break through that initial complacency and any tendency to procrastinate. But by initially resolving to do those three workouts a week, slowly building a habit one small step at a time, and honoring that habit, I eventually got to a healthy routine that strengthened my body, my mind, and most importantly my inner resolve.

Making that first effort can seem like a daunting prospect. It can take a little extra will power to break through the inertia of *not* having tried for a long while or the tendency to procrastinate. By keeping our mind's eye on the long-term benefit we will accrue, instead of focusing on the short-term discomfort or pain we think we'll have to go through, it can really help us get going.

By also starting small and gradually increasing, you make the effort regularly and are now on your way to having something to build on. With each thing you do, day by day, your inner resolve grows in strength and capacity. Before you know it, you are attempting and accomplishing things you never would have tried previously.

If you're still finding it difficult to get started, try making a list of all the ways you will benefit from getting it done, including how you will feel over the long term. Try to list out five or more benefits if possible. Then, list some ways your life will stay the same or get worse if you don't start. Use this as motivation and take that first small step to overcome the inertia of complacency. Remember to choose something small and easily obtainable that moves you closer to completing your task.

From there, continue to set easy, achievable next steps and complete them one by one on a comfortable timeline until you have finished the entire objective. You are now creating positive momentum and strengthening your resolve. Keep it going, don't let that inner muscle atrophy or your phone distract you. Build steadily from here by finding little challenges each day to complete.

Start with the easiest things first, build slowly from there, and before you know it, you'll be tackling big goals and big tasks without hesitation.

Tool #4: Use The Momentum of Daily Habits

Habits are exceptionally powerful and a fundamental building block for obtaining your desires and goals. By establishing daily habits, you can create a self-sustaining momentum that pulls you along in the direction you want to go.

This can be the case even when you wake up some mornings and don't feel like putting any effort into achieving your goals, which can happen to anyone for any reason. Sometimes, we feel tired, unmotivated, sick, or worried about something that consumes our mental resources. Or we can also get side-tracked, distracted, temporarily into something else, or tied up with other responsibilities. It happens to the most disciplined of us, and sometimes taking a day off is necessary.

That said, daily habits that we have been building for a long time, can provide us with a powerful momentum to help us to power around the obstacles that get in the way of our success. I have woken up countless times over my lifetime and not felt like exercising on a given day, or uninspired to get an outstanding task done. It again, happens to all of us.

More often than not, though, I get back to working on my goals because of a long-standing habit of working toward them daily. That is the power of daily habits—they generate their own momentum and drag us along even on those days when we don't feel like doing anything. You often don't even have to think about it; the habit strikes and you just get up and get to it.

Habits take time to build, but once they are firmly established, they can carry us quickly toward our goals and help us overcome any tendency to procrastinate and through the adversity of our most challenging days.

There is an older gentleman I know and admire named Fred who, at the time of writing this book, is in his mid-sixties. Fred is unique and decided about thirty-five years ago that he would run every single day of his life. He must have made a serious commitment to himself and developed an impressively powerful daily habit, because he never missed running at least five miles per day—for thirty-five years straight!

It didn't matter if it was extreme heat, rain or shine, snow or ice, or sleet or hail; you would see Fred every day, if you looked for him, with his running shoes slapped on and making his way around the neighborhood on his daily trek.

Eventually, Fred's historical streak of running was interrupted because of an accident that hospitalized him for several days, but he did get back to his routine. His amazing streak was documented in 2019, when he set the Canadian record for running in 34 consecutive Boston Marathons. Not many human beings can say they've surpassed this remarkable accomplishment.

While all that mileage eventually caught up with Fred, and he had to reduce his routine to one to two weekly runs, he still maintains this impressive commitment to running regularly for the rest of his life. Fred personifies the dedication of a warrior's mentality, and his extraordinary accomplishment reflects the power of desire and the momentum of a deeply entrenched and powerful life habit.

Warrior Mentality

In general, it's relatively safe to say that the harder you try, the more you do, and the more time you invest, the quicker the results will come and the better they will be. Of course, there can be exceptions, but it's no secret that if you are willing to take on hard things, you will strengthen your resolve, improve your discipline and capabilities, and increase your chances for long-term, sustainable success.

Let's borrow a little inspiration from a warrior mentality, which refers to a state of mind that personifies total commitment to a cause, passion, or purpose and the dedication to keep going through adversity.

Warrior mentality can be observed in many areas of life from athletes, to those dedicated to helping others, or in anyone with a goal they find exceptionally meaningful or important. Warriors, in this context, are completely committed to what they are working to achieve and there is no serious thought of ever quitting or giving up.

They are mentally tough and strong and expect challenging moments on their road to success. They're willing to endure through pain and discomfort to get where they want to go. They weather the storms, bounce back from setbacks, and use failure as an opportunity to learn, adjust, and keep going. They are relentless in the pursuit of their goals, and they don't let their doubts and fears, or those of others dissuade them. They choose to do things now instead of later, so they stay strong and carry on in the face of adversity.

If you have an "all in" state of mind, dedicated to following your passion and achieving your goals, then you have a warrior's mentality. The only things that will ever stop you are success (because you've achieved your goal) or failure. If it's the former, you'll pick up where you left off and establish a new goal, and if it's the latter, your temporary failure is only going to stop you until you adjust your approach and get back to it—like John did after his accident. We'll get more deeply into managing failure in Chapter 7.

If you're interested in building a warrior's mentality, then start by answering these questions:

- Are you absolutely clear about what you want?
- Are you willing to fully commit to achieving your goal and to give it your uninhibited, 100% effort?
- Do you have such a strong desire to achieve your goal that you are willing to do whatever it takes? (Without, of course, harming anyone in the process)

- Will you continue striving toward your goal in the face of adversity?
- Will you continue striving toward your goal in the face of unexpected setbacks?
- Will you continue striving toward your goal in the face of fear or failure?
- Will you work every day toward achieving your goal no matter what, even if you only have the time to devote a few minutes?

If you can answer *YES* to these questions, then you are well on your way to developing a warrior's mindset. Until then, stick to that "Dirty Discipline" until the time comes when you've established some daily habits aimed at achieving your goals.

Four Tools to Build Desire, Discipline, and the Power of your Personal Will:

Tool #1: Have Desire – the more intense the better

Tool #2: Dirty Discipline – use it as needed

Tool #3: Empower Your Personal Will – one small step at a time

Tool #4: Use the Momentum of Daily Habits

Now step back and congratulate yourself. You're now clear about what matters most to you and have empowered your personal will to help you get there. You know how to build useful habits, overcome procrastination, and have the first four mental skills of a high-performing mind. You're ready to move forward.

You'll need a few more tools, though, to ensure you don't get knocked off course by any challenging moments or setbacks on the way to achieving your goals. You'll want to be prepared and powerful enough to get around any obstacles you encounter. Let's find out exactly how next in Chapter 2.

Let's Make This Stick

1. Write down your primary desire or goal from the beginning of this Chapter:

_____

2. What small steps will you begin with to achieve this desire/ goal?

i. _____

ii. _____

iii. _____

3. What's one thing you can do **daily** to ensure you achieve this desire/ goal? In other words, what habits can you start building today?

_____

4. If you could choose one attribute of Warrior's Mentality, what would it be?

_____

CHAPTER 2

Did Someone Say It Was Supposed To Be Easy?

Building Resilience, and Overcoming Adversity

I remember being seventeen years old and driving my recently purchased, but very used and rusty black Volkswagen diesel, down a quiet country road on my way to school one day. I couldn't have been more excited—I had recently got my license, and it was my first ever car. I had just bought it from my mom, and I couldn't wait to drive my friends around after class.

On my way down a good-sized hill, not five minutes from home, something caught the corner of my eye. What I could have sworn looked a lot like a car wheel, sped by my driver-side window and bounced down the hill in front of me.

"Wait, it was a car wheel!"

I had the time to think about how strange this was and to wonder where the heck it could have come from before noticing the steering wheel getting harder to move. An instant later, the car tilted heavily to the left before coming to a slow, grinding and very lop-sided stop on the side of the road.

"What! That was MY car wheel?"

First shock and then disbelief as I got out and surveyed the damage. *Not that bad all things considered,* but there I was stuck out in the middle of nowhere, with a three-wheeled car, no phone, and no idea what to do. It was a rude awakening from my earlier daydreams of having fun with my friends as I drove them around town. I stood there stunned and stared at the rusty brake, where the wheel was supposed to be. Things were definitely not going to plan!

With a mood starting to match the color of the paint, I trudged grumpily down the rest of the hill in the direction of the nearest gas station to get a tow truck and call my parents. All I knew was I wanted the seven hundred bucks, I paid for the car, back from my mom!

There Will Be Hard Parts

Though it may not involve losing the front wheel of a car, safe to say we've all had times when something unexpected has come along and rewritten our plans. If we want to live an optimal life, then having the ability to keep going during challenging moments is a critical ingredient for success. How we respond to adversity can be the difference between achieving our goals and failure. Will we crumble into a crying heap on the hood of the car when a wheel falls off? Or will we pick ourselves up, accept our circumstances, and see what we can do to get back on the road as quickly as possible?

Hopefully, the part about accepting our circumstances and getting back on the road as quickly as possible is the inspiring choice. But what can we do to increase the chances *we will respond positively* when that first setback arrives or worse, when something more serious and unexpected happens in our lives?

There are three mental tools that will help us to respond in a high-performing way to the adversity we'll encounter as we strive to live our optimal lives, be at our best and achieve our goals.

Using these tools can help us find the solutions, inner strength, and resilience we'll need to get past any obstacles we encounter and to make the most of our circumstances. Let's find out what they are and how to use them next to vastly increase our chances of persevering through challenging moments and achieving our goals.

Tool #1: Expect Challenges

Our first mental tool is to simply remind ourselves (regularly) to **expect there will always be unforeseen challenges** in life. This might sound simple and perhaps a little negative, but by anticipating it could get hard at some point, we aren't taken by surprise when it does and are mentally ready to persevere through.

Using this mental tool regularly also helps us understand that challenging periods are a natural part of the process of achieving our goals. Rather than getting blind-sided by a setback and seeing it as proof we're doomed to fail or won't ever bounce back, we instead see it as a *learning experience* and an indication that it may be time to rethink our approach. By remembering there will be hard parts, we're more resilient and ready to act in a positive way to find solutions instead of panicking or giving up after we go through challenging moments or setbacks.

When I was in my mid-twenties, my friend Alex organized a group trip to go white water rafting. Knowing Alex was a bit of an adrenaline junkie made me a little nervous, but it sounded like a fun plan, so I decided to go. A week later, ten of us packed into two cars and made the four-hour drive to Red River, which apparently, according to Alex, was the best place around to go rafting. This should have been my first warning.

When we arrived, we found out that the rapids were at a season high that week, which was the last thing I wanted to hear. I had secretly been hoping it would be more the leisurely sort of adventure. Alex on the other hand was pumped, and especially when we found out the run we were about to go on had been closed the day before because the water was so rough. *Fantastic,* I thought to myself. *Just what a group of rookie rafters needs: Class 5 rapids!*

I listened extra attentively during the instructional talk we got from our French river guide Clément. This was partly because I couldn't understand half of what he said—due to his thick accent—and partly because *water safety* was suddenly a far more interesting subject than usual. I especially clued into one of his key points. "Eef anyting go wrong, and you fall out ze boat, jus stay cam and make sure you greep ze paddle." *What do you mean, IF we fall out of the boat?!* Aren't *we paying this guy to take us down the river safely?*

By this point my self-preservation system had woken up and was shouting, "Warning, warning!" I seriously contemplated heading back to the car. *Maybe I should just drive down and meet the group once they reach the bottom of the run?*

It was probably the peer pressure, but before I knew it, we were all getting into wet suits and being fitted for helmets and paddles. As we climbed into the raft, I looked ahead and saw the groups in front of us paddle leisurely away from the dock into relatively calm water. *Maybe I'm overthinking this,* I thought. *Yeah, there's a few rocks sticking out, but this looks reasonable, I can do this!* I reassured myself and relaxed a little. But prematurely it turns out.

We rounded the first bend and were greeted by rapids the size of cars. "This does NOT look good!" I shouted, but nobody could hear me over the roar of the water crashing over boulders.

My self-preservation system officially moved up into panic mode. I glanced back at the dock and contemplated my chances of making it if I abandoned ship and swam for it. It was clearly too late; there was no escape!

The first wave hit and a couple of people got knocked briefly out of their seats. Startled, a few of us made quick eye contact, but nervous laughter broke the tension. Alex, on the other hand, was smiling from ear to ear with what could only be described as a look of glee in his eyes. The rest of us had the look of something in our eyes too—terror as the next wave hit.

At this point, I was sure we were all going to die. I got about halfway through a prayer begging the river gods for mercy when a woman—who was supposed to be in the seat in front of me—suddenly flew backwards and knocked me and the poor guy seated behind us clear out of the boat. Apparently, we weren't alone and miraculously the only one of the ten of us who didn't fall out was our French river guide Clément. So much for the goal of not falling out of the boat! Plan B now in effect!

"Greep ze paddle and stay cam, greep ze paddle and stay cam" was now a mantra in my head as I plunged upside down under raging white water. As I came up, I couldn't see past the foaming waves but held onto my paddle with a death grip. Anyone nearby would have heard me as I floated by—between forced gulps of white foamy water—desperately shouting, "*Greep ze paddle, stay cam, stay cam...gasp...greep ze paddle. Cam, cam!!!*"

Turns out Clément was a genius and his words worked like a charm. I popped out—along with several others—a few hundred feet downriver where we were all pulled safely out of the water.

I didn't die, I didn't die! I was oddly elated by my new found low-standard for success. Clément had also become a folk-hero to our group for some reason, despite it being ambiguous just how much he "*helped*" us get down that run. If there was ever a next time, apparently, we should specify that when he "leads" us down again, it has to be *in* the boat.

Tool #2: Pre-Plan Constructive Responses

Having our own version of "Greep ze paddle and stay cam," can mean the difference between success and failure. **Expect Challenges** was our first tool for being more resilient and mentally prepared to respond in a positive way if we fell out of the boat. Clément provided us with our **second tool: Pre-Plan Construc-**

tive Responses. By giving us clear instructions to stay calm and hang onto our paddles ahead of time, *if* we fell out of the boat, we had a *constructive response* prepared when things didn't go as expected.

Having a plan—no matter how simple—can be critical for ensuring we don't panic when that first wave of adversity hits as we try to reach our goals. It pre-loads our brains to focus on *what needs to be done to succeed instead of how wrong everything seems to be going.* This enables us to *respond constructively* instead of *responding self-destructively* with unhelpful negative reactions or giving up prematurely.

If I didn't have a plan as I got knocked out of the boat that day, I might have panicked at a bad time, like when I was submerged, and made matters far worse for myself.

When we're prepared, it's easier to avoid *self-destructive* responses and believing there's no way to succeed. When we expect challenges, it's easier to find *constructive responses* and look for a way around obstacles so we can keep moving forward toward achieving our goals. We understand obstacles are just part of the process and avoid unhelpful negative reactions.

Not Having a Plan Makes Things Harder

I never anticipated having to go through the debilitating health challenge I described in the introduction. I knew it happened to people, but I reasoned that I had a healthy diet and kept myself in good shape so thought I would avoid anything like that. Clearly, I was wrong.

Shock and denial was my natural response, particularly in those first couple of months. I couldn't believe something like that could happen to me, so I struggled to accept my circumstances. Consequently, I suffered emotionally from depression for a period because I didn't have any coping strategies or constructive responses yet, like immediately searching for ways to improve my circumstances.

After many weeks of despair, I eventually got to a mental place where I developed a more positive mindset and found some constructive responses. I started researching my condition, monitoring what I ate, and working towards solutions to improve my circumstances by developing a diet to manage my illness.

Preparing ahead of time isn't always possible; some things will just take us by surprise no matter what, and we'll get more into those later in this chapter. But when we can, planning for the worst can go a long way in helping us through challenging moments.

Prepare Constructive Responses Ahead of Time and Build Resilience

Having an Emergency Response Plan at work (or at home) in the event of a fire, or some other urgent event, is common practice. It helps us to have predetermined actions in place, so we respond in a positive way. The goal of *A High-Performing Mind* is to ensure we don't hesitate, or worse, stop and quit prematurely when we hit those unexpected setbacks. We want to adjust and keep going right away instead. By planning constructive responses *ahead of time,* we can help ensure we respond constructively when we need to.

There are times when coming up with a plan for how to respond constructively will be straightforward. When we fall out of a raft into the water, for example, being prompted to hang on to our paddle and remain calm is a simple and obvious constructive response to survive.

Ultimately, our goal—when we encounter adversity—is to respond positively in a higher-performing way, which is in our long-term best interests. "Oh yeah, that's right, something challenging was supposed to happen when I try to achieve this goal. Okay, this is the moment I'm supposed to make an adjustment in my approach and keep going."

Aside from situations where it's near impossible to predict what could go wrong or what challenging circumstances we may have to face, there may be times when we can anticipate many of the challenges we're likely to experience. These might occur during things like exams, presentations, competitions, job interviews, or difficult conversations, where we are familiar with many of the dynamics we will encounter.

For example, a while back, I worked with an athlete named Ben who was the second-best player in his country in his sport. Given his ranking, he was often in a position of having to play opponents ranked below him, but rarely ever lost in these situations.

Ben's secret was that he always expected it would be hard to win no matter how many times he had defeated an opponent in the past. He was also a master at mentally preparing for all the different challenges he might face during matches. We would usually talk through scenarios before a tournament to make sure that he was resilient and would respond constructively to anything that came up during competition.

"Your opponent might have improved and be harder to beat than when you last played." I might say.

"I'm ready for that possibility and am prepared to work harder to win than last time," Ben would respond.

We also would get into specifics. "There might be moments where you get really tired and feel like giving up."

Ben's reply would be, "I'll prepare for the possibility of feeling really tired and when that happens, I will take some extra time between points and remember that I have trained hard and I will recover soon. I expect that at some point I will feel like giving up and I will remind myself to stay calm and refocus on my plan and strategy to win. This will help me to stay positive and keep going without letting down."

"There might also be some bad calls you'll have to deal with from the referee." I'd say.

"I'll take a deep breath if that happens and use a bad call as a reminder to refocus on my game plan and my goal to win," he'd say.

By planning *constructive responses* like these for each situation, Ben was exceptionally resilient through challenging moments and able to perform at a higher level consistently. He was able to stay focused on his goal of winning without getting distracted by negative situations, thoughts, and emotions when it mattered most. Resilience increases when we're mentally prepared for potential adversity.

Going Through Hard Things Makes Us Stronger

If you only do what's easy, it will feel hard to succeed.

One key concept I've used successfully in coaching people in any field over the years to perform at their best is to ensure the difficulty of practice or preparation exceeds the difficulty of "performance-time" whenever possible. The reasoning is simple: if practice is harder than the moment we need to perform, then it will feel easier to succeed and results will be better when it counts.

If you're prepping for an exam, for example, then making sure you know all the material and testing yourself with harder questions than the ones you expect to encounter on the test will pay dividends. Similarly, if training for a half marathon race, then running five miles further or with a 10lb weight on your back during practice, will make race-day seem a lot easier without these extra challenges in place.

People who exercise regularly are no doubt familiar with this concept. Doing something strenuous like lifting weights or running may fatigue us in the short term, but in the long run our bodies adapt to the increased load, and we get stronger and more capable. When we're fit, we don't get tired as quickly, and our daily physical tasks can feel easy by comparison.

Similarly, as unpleasant as difficult situations are, they also illustrate that there can be unforeseen silver linings from going through difficult things. I may not have anticipated the health crisis I went through, but over time, it became clear that I became mentally stronger and more resilient from the experience. Getting seriously ill can be traumatic and frightening. It can leave us feeling like life isn't worth living and wondering if we'll ever be able to recover and be happy again.

If we persevere, though, we can develop the confidence to find our way through any challenge. People who've overcome debilitating experiences often speak of gaining a more balanced perspective and being better able to recognize what's truly important in life. People who have gone through intense hardship often talk about no longer being bothered by things that previously caused them stress, or worry, and feeling more empathy and compassion for others. Difficult life-altering experiences can be humbling and exact a heavy toll, but they can leave our hearts and minds in a better place once we've had the time to heal.

Though all very different, the above situations highlight that **going through hard things makes us stronger.** It can be a real challenge when we hit serious adversity for the first time. It's natural to feel low, a sense of loss, that life is unfair, or will never be good again.

Once we've had some time to process our situation and allow these negative feelings to run their course, we can start to try and find more positive responses to our circumstances. As difficult as things can get, it's helpful to remember that going through them can make us higher performing human beings. Adversity can reset our perspective and strengthen our minds, and life can feel easier because we have learned to cope with so much more.

Getting Blindsided - Dealing with Unexpected Adversity

Sometimes, it's not just about our goals and we have to overcome much more serious and difficult circumstances. Sometimes, life blindsides us with things that turn our world upside down and into disarray. In those moments, we're asked to manage, somehow and in some way, through unexpected and life-altering adversity.

This was certainly the case for my brother John when he turned twenty-four years old. I'll never forget the day he called and asked to come over saying he wanted to tell me something important.

I was worried right away. John rarely asked to come over, we were close, but didn't hang out that often at that time outside of family get-togethers. I'd also never known John to say something serious like this, he was my risk taking, adventure loving younger brother, and he was living his life, doing his thing, and everything seemed fine from the outside. Why would he want to talk to me in person all of a sudden, I wondered?

Well, I didn't have to wait long to find out. John, who lived about ten minutes away from me in Montreal then, came by my apartment shortly after he called. I let him in and we headed over to the kitchen to talk. He seemed somber, which only served to make me more concerned.

He paused before looking up, the strain of what he was about to tell me was etched in his eyes. He went on to tell me he hadn't been feeling physically well for a while in an unfamiliar and unsettling way, so he finally went to the doctor to get things checked out. He then told me he'd been diagnosed with cancer—and that it was already quite progressed. He had stage IV Hodgkin's disease and had three tumors including a seven-inch one in his chest. He went on to tell me that he would be having surgery right away and that he would be starting chemotherapy and radiation immediately after at a local hospital.

I was blindsided by the news and devastated for John. Nothing like this had ever happened to any of us in our immediate family. We were fortunate to have had a very positive upbringing in a loving household that enjoyed good health and happy times. Outside of the divorce of our parents at age sixteen and the death of our family dog, who got hit by a car shortly after, we never really had to go through anything this serious and difficult before.

Hearing news like this from my brother shook me to my core. He was a pillar in my life, which I unconsciously knew on the surface, but only truly understood in that moment when one of those foundational pillars was suddenly hit and threatening to crumble.

We both cried in the moment he told me. Both of us scared for John's future. We didn't know or fully understand what this diagnosis meant for his survival and what his life would look like in the immediate future.

On the good news side of the equation, my brother John was fortunate to have an unshakable inner resolve. Although deeply concerned, he never hesitated for a moment to face this unexpected challenge head-on and do whatever was necessary to get through and recover. And that's what he did.

John went through this challenge like a champion. He didn't hesitate for a moment or waste a lot of time feeling sorry for himself. Without missing a beat, he got on with the business of overcoming his cancer. He instantly focused his entire being and energy on doing anything and everything he could think of to get past the disease and back to his normal life in good health and as quickly as possible.

In the weeks ahead, John had open chest surgery to remove the large tumors that had grown so quickly and aggressively and then underwent six rounds of chemotherapy, followed by radiation. In addition to the medical treatments, John also explored other ways to improve his chances for recovery including cleaning up his lifestyle, taking steps to establish a much healthier diet, exploring and trying some alternative health options, and ensuring there was nothing in his environment at work or at home, which could contribute to the growth of cancer cells. He read books, educated himself, and found a path forward of doing everything he could to help heal his body.

Throughout the entire time, John, an entrepreneur since he finished university, kept building his business and the rest of his life going. I would go to visit him at the hospital while he was doing his chemo treatments. There he'd be, hooked up to an IV and working away on his computer like everything was normal despite being in a hospital gown and living there for weeks at a time.

John was fortunate to get past his cancer quickly. The operation and treatments had been a success, and his tumors were gone. We all breathed a collective sigh of relief when he was told he was in remission and was able to put this first chapter of serious adversity in his life behind him.

John is a truly remarkable person. When I did my speech about him, as his best man at his wedding several years later, one of the main themes was about his incredible resilience. No matter what happens to John, he finds a way to stay positive through the darkest times. He has an inspiring resolve and spends very little, if any time, dwelling on his problems, and quickly moves into finding and focusing on solutions.

This brings us to our **third tool**, which we can all use during setbacks and challenging times. **Acknowledge problems, but quickly find and focus on solutions.**

Perspective Is Everything

You don't have to go through a life crisis for something to be hard. Adversity can show up at any time in our daily lives. From having to get up early to exercise or practice, or prepare for a big exam, an important presentation, or job interview, to having an unexpected confrontation with someone, to experiencing the end of a relationship or losing a job, there are all kinds of ways that life can challenge us.

When something difficult happens unexpectedly to me at this point in my life, I often remind myself that *I've been here before and I will get through this*. When it also impacts me emotionally, I often respond internally with *Yes, I feel terrible now, but this will pass.*

These two responses remind us that we've been through many challenging circumstances in the past and that we can cope through again. We know we've done it before so have the confidence that we can get through. They can help us stay mentally strong and resilient when it matters most.

One of my favorite quotes has always been, "It's not how far you fall, but how high you bounce." We all fall at some point, but let's choose to bounce back up and keep going so we can fly again in the future.

Adversity has the potential to make us stronger. It can broaden our understanding of what can happen and what can go wrong. It makes us a little wiser and can help us see the flaws in our plans. It can help us understand what we might need to improve and make the way forward a little clearer.

Anytime we make it through something hard, there's the potential for everything else to feel a lot easier by comparison—at least for a while. But again, it comes down to how we choose to respond. Will we give in to fear, close ourselves off to life and not find a way forward? Or will we find a way to persevere and rise again so we can enjoy our life in new ways?

Adversity is almost certain to come along at some point. By focusing on solutions as quickly as possible, and knowing we will respond positively if it does, we're mentally stronger, more resilient, and able to keep going until we succeed.

It won't be easy or always straightforward and we may get knocked-down many times, but if we use our three tools from this chapter, we give ourselves the best chance to find higher-performing responses, ensure we persevere, and make the most of any situation.

Three Tools To Build Strength, Resilience and Manage Pressure:

Tool #1: Expect challenges

Tool #2: Pre-plan constructive responses

Tool #3: Acknowledge problems, but quickly find and focus on solutions

We've now completed the second stage of our climb up the hill to a High-Performing Mind. We have some new tools to help us through any adversity that comes our way so that we have the ability to keep going—if the going gets tough—and we can still make it to the top. We should also have better insight into the secrets of success for high performers and the things they do to have a strong and resilient mind.

There's another important tool that you'll need right away to exponentially improve your foundation to succeed by ensuring you have an empowering attitude. Let's find out exactly what that is next in Chapter 3.

Let's Make This Stick

1. Write down your primary desire from Chapter 1:

_____

2. List at least three struggles, worries, or challenges you could potentially encounter before achieving this goal:

i. _____

ii. _____

iii. _____

3. Plan your constructive responses. What will you do to respond positively to your circumstances?

i. _____

ii. _____

iii. _____

4. List at least one way you could personally benefit from each of the three struggles you listed above. Are there any positives? Will you be stronger from going through them? Will you be wiser the next time?

i. _____

ii. _____

iii. _____

iv. _____

v. _____

CHAPTER 3

Always Do Your Best-

Even If the Fish Dies

Our neighbor's son across the road had a beautiful purple and white tropical Betta fish he named "Thomas and Friends." I guess that's what happens when you let a four-year-old name the family pet. Whenever they traveled, they'd usually ask us to look after him, and even though we weren't "fish people" per se, we happily took him in.

I learned quickly there was more to a fish than I initially thought. It surprised me how in the mornings, like clockwork, he'd swim around and get excited before mealtime, just like a dog. We took turns feeding him, and the kids especially looked forward to our little Betta buddy's occasional visits.

Just before our third or fourth stint of fish-sitting, our neighbor, who was rushing to catch a flight, dropped by one afternoon with the tank in hand looking upset.

"Sorry guys, I have no idea what's wrong with him. He looks sick or something and might be dying, but I'm super late and have

to get to the airport." She handed him over and dashed home, apologizing as she left.

We brought him into the kitchen and huddled around his little aquarium. She was right, Thomas and Friends did NOT look good! He was pale, his usual vibrant colors were muted, and his ordinarily impressive mane of flowing fins was tattered and had receded since we last saw him.

After staring at him for a while, with no idea what to do, I did a little research to see if we could figure out what was wrong with him. After comparing him to a couple of pictures we found online, it turned out he had something called "fin-rot," which was seemingly quite advanced.

Not a good prognosis for Thomas and Friends! He needed immediate help if he was going to make it.

The research called for a "hospital quarantine tank," saltwater treatments, and something called "Indian almond leaf" to help stop the infection. The almond leaf sounded a little exotic, but if that was what would save little Thomas and Friends, then so be it!

My wife gaped at me, "Seriously?! This sounds like a lot of work for a seven-dollar fish. Look at him, there's no way he's going to make it."

We both glanced at Thomas and Friends who was now floating listlessly on his side. He wasn't making a good case for himself.

"So, what are we supposed to do?" I asked. "Just tell the neighbor's kid, umm sorry, but the fish didn't look like he was going to make it, so we flushed him down the toilet?!"

"Alright," she agreed reluctantly. "But you're on your own for this one." And off she went to do actual practical things instead.

The more I researched what to do, the more complicated things became. On top of the quarantine tank, the salt treatments, and the almond leaf, I had to do daily water changes and keep him at 78 degrees so he wouldn't feel "distressed," the website told me.

The meat thermometer I stuck into the tank to check the temperature thirty times a day probably didn't help his nerves any, but more importantly the water was only 71 degrees. "Well, we can't have him distressed while he's trying to recover," I thought to myself.

Not having a tank heater and not sure what else to do, I placed him in his hospital tank (a converted flower vase), then set that into a cooking pot filled with water. I then placed the whole thing on the warming-burner of our stove.

My wife's eyes narrowed when she saw the arrangement. She wasn't nearly as impressed with the solution as I was. I conceded that cooking meals might be a little trickier for a while, but reiterated, "It's for a good cause."

Unfortunately, this arrangement also needed some explaining to the babysitter. I had to assure her we weren't, in fact, cooking the fish alive, so she wasn't scandalized when she came over to watch the kids.

There's no doubt the whole fish-on-the-stove thing looked questionable. It was also hard to tell how Thomas and Friends felt about being so close to a sizzling frying pan around dinner time. But as far as I was concerned, all that mattered was that we reached the recommended tropical temperatures in his tank so he could recover.

I woke up the next day eager to see how our patient was doing. I darted down stairs to the kitchen. The temperature had—fortunately—reached the desired 78 degrees. I was relieved I hadn't accidentally cooked him overnight but was now concerned because Thomas and Friends looked way worse. There were pieces of detached fin floating around and he was lying near the bottom of the tank hardly moving at all.

The kids and I were worried, but not knowing what else to do, I continued the process. I changed his salt water daily, gave him the almond leaf, and kept him fed and warm on the stove. We came down on day three fearing the worst, but miraculously Thomas and Friends somehow wasn't dead and by day four, he actually looked a little better!

All the effort was starting to seem worthwhile. By day seven, he appeared to have energy back and on day ten, it seemed like he was going to make it. His fins were nowhere near their previous billowy standards, but his color was definitely better, and he seemed like his old self again.

We did it! We saved Thomas and Friends! The kids were happy, and the wife even bought me a T-shirt with a picture of a Betta fish and a human fist-bumping. I was the family hero… for about a day…

Rookie mistake apparently. It turns out we celebrated too soon. One morning, a few days later, we woke up to find poor old Thomas and Friends floating dead at the top of his tank. I was gutted but wasn't sure if it was more because I missed the little guy, or all the lost hours and the hundred and four dollars I spent trying to keep him alive.

As suspected, our neighbor friend didn't lose any sleep after we told her the news about Thomas and Friends swimming his way into fish heaven, but we all worried how her son would handle it. He was only four years old at the time and it was, after all, his pet and had lived in his room his whole life. She finally decided to break the news to him a couple of weeks later, we all agonized how he was going to take it. "Honey, I'm really sorry to tell you this, but Thomas and Friends didn't make it and he's now in fish heaven."

He shrugged, unconcerned. "Really? Meh, can I have a Gatorade?"

Tool #1: Always Doing Your Best

I get it. A lot of effort for *evidently* not much return on investment, so why all the rigmarole for a dying fish? Well, a few reasons. Aside from not wanting the neighbor's pet to die on our watch and a general care for the well-being of all living creatures, my sometimes inconvenient habit of always trying to do the best I can decided to get involved.

It would be a fair question, at this point, to wonder how spending nearly three weeks of time and effort, only to have the fish die in the end, could possibly be a good sales pitch for always doing your best?

The truth is, we do the best we can for ourselves. Sure, we might use our tool for this chapter: Build the habit to **always do your best**—in part for the fish, or whatever our current challenge, but the reality is that our best can benefit anyone. Including ourselves.

Before we dive a little further into that last statement, let's back up for a minute and point out the obvious. The idea of *always doing your best* isn't a new concept. You've likely heard this numerous times before. It's a common go-to line when someone we care for is about to do something important that matters to them.

The phrase "do your best" can be taken in a variety of ways. There's the literal version that generally refers to bringing our best effort or performance to what we are about to do: "Don't forget to do your best." It can also be used to encourage someone who is nervous or worried about how things will go: "Don't worry, just do your best." It can also be meant as a reminder that we've done everything we can to prepare, and the outcome is now out of our hands: "All you can do is your best."

Growing up, my dad's number one piece of advice to me as a kid was about my effort level and he usually went with some version of "remember to work hard." My dad's main point was that if I gave it my full effort, I would perform better and hence enjoy myself more. He would remind me of this lesson often before sports, tests, and in pretty much any situation where I wanted to do well.

It's hard to fault the argument for bringing our best effort to the things that matter to us. There probably aren't many scenarios where *not trying* would lead to an optimal outcome or strengthen our capabilities. It's safe to say that nobody wins a gold medal, graduates top of their class, or becomes CEO of a successful business without a long-established habit of always bringing their best to everything they do.

Whether it's an athlete, business leader, artist, chef, musician, or someone wanting to get the most out of an important relationship, always doing our best is a sure way to get better results.

The one thing that all high performers I've worked with have in common is that no matter what they are doing, they strive to always bring their best to the equation. That means bringing complete dedication, focus, and effort to the task at hand and using their full physical, mental, and emotional skill sets to succeed.

Building the habit of always doing your best is a key element of developing a High-Performing Mind. Giving this a try will help you on your journey to having a High-Performing Mind. Let's explore some situations where we might be challenged to bring our best to the equation.

Tool #2: Give Your Full Effort Even If You Might Fail

When I was a kid, I always tried my best no matter what. I never thought about it, I just dove into whatever activity I was doing and gave it my 100% effort. It never occurred to me to do it another way. I'm not sure if this was because of my dad's consistent messaging to always work hard or just the way I was wired.

An athlete I worked with named Nathan on the other hand, had a different approach. He was exceptionally talented, but anytime he started to lose, he would visibly stop trying to win. I couldn't understand why for the longest time. "Why not keep running hard and see if you can make a comeback or at least figure out what you need to improve to win in the future?" I'd ask, trying to help him past this mental block.

Over time, I started to piece together that Nathan subconsciously preferred to *not try* and lose, rather than to be seen *trying* and having to admit his opponent was better than him. He was more afraid to fail and look like he was the weaker player than be seen as giving it his best effort and still losing. Nathan's unwillingness to put himself on the line, unfortunately, only served to weaken his mind and resolve and hold him back from reaching his full potential.

We can't always control or guarantee if we'll succeed, but we can control how much effort we give. If we allow fear of failing to stop us from trying, we'll never find out if we could have succeeded. By giving 100%, even when we're afraid to fail, we ensure we get the most out of ourselves and the situation we're in. Even if things don't work out, we still have the opportunity to identify what we need to improve in order to succeed the next time around.

Someone with a High-Performing Mind doesn't hold anything back because of the prospect of failing or looking bad. They go for it and give it their best shot, which maximizes their chances of achieving the success they envision in the long-run.

Do We Have the Habit? What's Your Level of Effort?

Hopefully by now you are familiar with the benefits of always doing your best. The important question is: do you have the habit of doing it? Is the attitude of doing your best so infused into your DNA that it happens automatically, even without thinking about it? It's important at this point to mention that the *habit of doing your best should not be confused with perfectionism.* The latter is a mentally unhealthy fixation that brings a diminishing return on our investment. If you are aiming to bring your best to the important things in your life however, you are on the right path to creating a more ideal life experience for yourself.

It might seem like a daunting prospect to always do your best, but the more often you do, the more areas of our lives that will benefit. If you're not used to giving your best, then this habit will feel hard those first few times you attempt to give more effort. But the more consistently you do your best, the easier it gets and the more natural it feels.

I worked with a young athlete named Ellie who usually only gave about a 4 out of 10 effort during practice. I explained to her how this meant she could only expect a 4 out of 10 rate of improvement and, similarly, 4 out of 10 results in competition. After understanding she could improve faster and get better results from herself, she agreed to improve her effort and intensity.

In the coming weeks, Ellie aimed to get her intensity up to a 5 out of 10 effort, then eventually a 6 out of 10. It was a challenge for her to make the change and to get the new habit of *trying harder* to stick. With consistent attempts to do her best each time she practiced or competed, she slowly started to make the new higher effort level a habit.

After several months, Ellie got up to an 8 out of 10 effort level in both practice and competition. This level became her new normal and she pointed out that sustaining the habit wasn't nearly as difficult as building it up.

I had a similar situation with an employee of mine named Gavin who I was also friends with outside of work. His effort for producing good quality work was often low and didn't meet our organization's high standards for customer service.

Over time, it became a source of contention between us, since I was ultimately accountable for the work his department produced. I did my best to coach Gavin so he could improve his effort and get better feedback from clients. My feedback didn't always go over well, and he made the occasional remark suggesting I was too picky about details that weren't a big deal in the grand scheme of things. Over time, Gavin's performance did noticeably improve, which was a relief, but not long after, he moved on to a new job.

Fortunately, our friendship survived and we still kept in touch. A couple of years after he switched jobs, I got a call from Gavin. He told me how he really appreciated working with me those years before and being exposed to the high standards we set. He told me how his clients and co-workers at his new place of work were really impressed with his performance. He credited his time spent working with us those years before with his high standards for his work.

Once we get used to always doing our best, it can become our new habit and feel as natural as our previously lower effort level felt.

Aiming to Do Our Best

As we saw with Ellie and Gavin, when we set the bar high and aim to do our best, it eventually becomes our new normal. It may take a little time to build the habit of always bringing our best to what we do, but when we do, we are able to live a more rewarding life. Bringing our best helps our lives go more smoothly in a variety of ways:

- We won't often have to face tough questions about our performance from ourselves or others.
- People appreciate our care and attention.
- We are able to achieve a higher level of success in whatever we set our minds to.
- Most importantly, we feel better about who we are.

The opposite is also true; when we have low standards, it becomes our normal. Learning to bring better effort to our actions can be a slow and arduous process. But not giving it our all can create a host of issues that we will have to face down the road, which can then lead to far more work to clean up. When we don't try our best, we create unnecessary adversity for ourselves that we will eventually have to face, including increased failure, unachieved ambitions, and disappointing people who are relying on us. Mediocre effort only ever leads to mediocre results.

Not doing our best can also mean missing out on our opportunity to feel a sense of accomplishment or satisfaction when we know we have done something well. Instead, when we don't give it our all, there is potential for feeling bad about *not* having done a good job; we know in the back of our minds that we could have done more.

These lingering negative sentiments about ourselves can stick with us emotionally. Over the long term, not doing our best doesn't give us a lot to feel good about, which can eventually have a negative impact on our confidence and sense of self-esteem.

Our Primary Relationship

Let's get back to our story about Thomas and Friends. I tried hard to save him not only because I cared about his well-being, but also because we do our best for ourselves. When things don't go as planned, if we know we've done all we can, it's easier to forgive ourselves and let go of our failures. Even when a neighbor's fish dies on your watch.

Always doing our best also helps us let go of our past mistakes, which consequently ensures that our sense of well-being isn't pulled down by regrets or dissatisfaction with who we are.

As my story about Thomas and Friends illustrates, the habit of always doing our best is, at times, inconvenient. There's no denying that it would have been easier to give up on Thomas and Friends before spending all that time and money. It's not always *convenient* to do our best, but it's worth it because there's a higher probability for success. In addition, by doing everything I could to help him, it was easier to forgive myself when things didn't work out. If I hadn't tried, I might have regretted it, knowing I could have done more to help.

At the end of the day, we are accountable to ourselves. You are the one you will wake up to in the morning, live with all day, and face before going to sleep at night.

By always doing the best you can, you nurture this all-important *primary relationship*. You can know that you are doing everything you can to make yourself happy, feel good about who you are, and forgive yourself when things don't work out the way you hope.

When we have the habit to always do our best, we not only maximize our chances for success, we feel better about ourselves and who we are. By doing the best we can, whether it involves trying to save a dying fish or trying to excel in an important part of our lives, no matter the outcome, we'll benefit in the long run.

Summary of Tools:

Tool #1: Always Do Your Best

Tool #2: Give your full effort, even if you might fail

Let's Make This Stick

1. Identify an area of your life that would benefit if you made more effort:

_____

2. What would change for the better if you did your best in this area of your life? What does always doing your best look like in this area of your life? List below how your actions would change if you tried your best and what more you could do:

_____

3. Identify a goal that you need to bring your best effort to:

_____

4. List three actions you can take to do more and bring your best effort to help you achieve this goal.

i. _____

ii. _____

iii. _____

CHAPTER 4

Openness and Self-Honesty

Accelerating Personal Growth and Improvement

In 1984, Mike Wallace, a famous American journalist and correspondent for the highly popular news magazine *60 Minutes*, sought medical help for his battle with depression. His doctor at the time told him to "forget the word depression, because that will be bad for your image." He would end-up carrying his secret for another twenty-one years.

In 2005, he finally made news of his own when he opened up about his personal difficulties with depression in his memoir, *Between You and Me*. Fortunately, awareness about mental illness has come a long way over the last thirty-five plus years.

The courage and honesty of a variety of well-known public figures, Mike Wallace included, has contributed to the gradual breakdown of the stigma surrounding mental health. Some of the most recognizable people on the planet— from Oprah Winfrey to Adele, Ryan Reynolds, Michael Phelps, and Lady Gaga, to name just a few— have acknowledged experiencing mental and emotional health struggles at times.

This openness and honesty has inspired many others to reveal their own personal burdens, which has included being marginalized and made to feel inadequate. This has paved the way for a growing understanding, tolerance, and empathy in society for those who have similarly suffered. Consequently, millions of people around the world are more likely to receive the acceptance, help, and support they need and deserve to be open and honest about who they are and their struggles. By no means do we live in a perfect world. Many are still treated unfairly, but at least there are signs we are moving in the right direction.

Over my business career, I was fortunate to work with a few brave individuals who were also open about their mental health and other challenges they were facing. Not only was their honesty inspiring, it helped management to better understand and support them. As a result, we were able to find ways to help them succeed in their work rather than inadvertently setting them up for failure.

As a high-performance coach, it was quickly evident that openness and honesty were key factors for a person to succeed and maximize their rate of progress toward achieving their goals. If someone wasn't open about their weaknesses or what was really holding them back, it was far more difficult to identify the areas they had to improve and to understand what they needed to achieve the success they wanted.

If we are interested in improving ourselves so we can get the results we are looking for and enjoy greater success and our lives more, then being honest about our weaknesses, or the things we need to change or develop, will help us achieve this far more quickly.

If we have a skill or ability that isn't up to par yet, or there's something that's holding us back in a significant way from succeeding and having the life we want, then it may be time for a change.

Tool #1: Acknowledge Your Weaknesses- Your Opportunity for Accelerated Growth and Greater Success

There's a formula I like to reference when working with people to inspire them to acknowledge their deficiencies: If you improve your biggest weakness, you get the greatest amount of positive change at the fastest possible rate. The choice becomes simple: Do you want to improve and get better results faster? Or do you want to ignore or deny what's holding you back and continue to repeat the same mistakes and miss out on the success you really want?

If we choose to go for better results, the challenge is finding the courage to honestly look at our actions and behaviors that might be easier to deny and sweep under the rug. High-Performing Minds are open to change and acknowledge their shortcomings so they can maximize their rate of improvement. They prioritize self-development and the potential for greater levels of success and fulfillment.

When we acknowledge our weaknesses, we give ourselves the opportunity for accelerated growth. We can only start working on a deficiency once we are aware of it and acknowledge that it exists. It can be difficult to admit that we need to improve something, but if we can focus on the personal benefits we will accrue by changing the way we behave, it becomes easier to accept.

I was fortunate to be born with a body that was quick and had good endurance. It was the foundation for a large part of any success I had when competing in sports. On the other hand, I didn't always pick up some of the hand-eye skills as easily. I had to work a little harder at those and practice often to get them up to the standards I needed them to be at to achieve some of my main goals.

I can certainly recall not being able to execute some of those hand-eye skills consistently enough at critical times during competition and losing some important matches because my accuracy wasn't up to par. Noticing this initially eroded my confidence to finish things off strongly and decisively when it mattered. I would tighten up and make errors too often for my liking.

I didn't flat-out deny there were things in my game that I had to address, but I didn't like thinking about it either, because it made me feel inadequate and that I didn't have enough talent to improve. I also didn't like it if someone else ever commented on any of my weaknesses—even when well-meaning. It usually made me feel defensive and insecure.

Unfortunately, for the longest time, this unwillingness to admit this specific deficiency to myself and prioritize working on it, only served to block me from the success I wanted.

This dynamic—of not acknowledging a weakness I knew I had—lasted until I was competing this one time at the National Championships. I was playing a match against a player who had previously been ranked as high as number 50 in the world—well above my level. I was having one of those rare moments of being in "the zone" and playing at my absolute best. To my surprise, and likely those watching, I took a two-sets to one lead. It looked like I might win the match.

Unfortunately, though, it wasn't meant to be. The next two sets didn't progress the way I hoped. I made some errors at crucial moments, again, due to some of those inconsistent skills. As things went on, I got more and more frustrated, and mistakes and lapses crept increasingly into my game. I watched as my commanding lead slowly evaporated. He came back and won narrowly in the fifth and final set.

When the match finished, I felt completely dejected. I had such a golden opportunity to win and was so close, but let it slip away. I was angry at myself for failing and for those specific skills letting me down once again.

On the good news side of the equation though, this loss was a major catalyst for me. I resolved then and there—as I sat by myself stewing in my frustration long after the match had ended—that I would do everything and anything I could to make the needed improvements to my game.

That summer, on top of all my usual training, I devoted an extra two hours daily to working on those specific weaknesses that I felt had contributed to my losing that day. The improvement didn't come overnight, but it slowly got better over time.

I'm grateful I made the most of losing that day and acknowledged my weaknesses could no longer be ignored. I finally chose improvement and self-development over my unwillingness to address what I always knew was holding me back. These decisions and the extra time and effort paved the way for greater success and enjoyment in the years ahead.

Tool #2: Prioritize Self-Development Over Denying Flaws

It's easy to let the knee-jerk reaction of denying our flaws and weaknesses be our initial response when confronted with uncomfortable observations about our behavior or performance. There's no doubt it's harder to face the truth sometimes about what we may need to change or improve. If we take the time to consider the potential rewards to the overall quality of our lives, it makes the effort, discomfort, and chafed emotions of an honest inner assessment worthwhile. We just need to be willing to yank off that Band-Aid and admit how we need to change, where we might have gone wrong, or how we could improve when we aren't happy with our circumstances or results.

When I was in my early twenties, my brother candidly told me that my expectations for people were too high and unreasonable at times. I expected ideal responses from people, particularly family members, and wasn't understanding when they didn't behave that way.

The feedback stung and my first reaction was to be defensive about my brother's observations and deny there might be some truth to it. Eventually, once I stopped protecting my pride, I became more open to the information. I was able to acknowledge this was something I could improve. I was then able to notice times where I did have unreasonable expectations and correct my thinking in the moment.

By being aware of this tendency to have unrealistic expectations of people, I was able to become more realistic and accepting of others (and of myself as a by-product). This eventually led to better relationships with friends and family, which was well worth the discomfort of listening to my brother's feedback and making the effort to change my behavior.

Admitting Flaws Shows Strength Not Weakness

Legendary basketball icon Kobe Bryant often spoke about how he coached his athletes to study past game videos, particularly of times where they didn't perform well. As unpleasant as that might have been for them, it helped them spot weaknesses and see a clear path to take their games to the next level.

When someone points out a behavior that isn't working, it's an opportunity for us to ask ourselves openly and honestly if we agree and if it's something we can improve. If it is, and we decide to make the change, it's an opportunity, and the payoff is increased long-term life enjoyment.

Being open and honest about needed changes also helps us let go of the past and what's holding us back. It can be liberating to acknowledge our shortcomings, because it means we have things we can improve and that we're not doomed to continuously repeat mistakes. Like Mike Wallace, if we're struggling in some way, admitting it to others can help us find the support we need to overcome our challenges.

I worked with a McGill University team in Canada many years back. One team member named Madison, who had struggled all season in pressure situations, pulled me aside minutes before the semifinals of the season ending college championships. She had made no mention of it prior to that moment, but suddenly admitted to feeling intensely anxious and worried about letting her teammates down. She described being so petrified to lose, she couldn't think straight and felt physically ill.

It was a classic case of pre-game nerves, though perhaps intensified given the significance of the moment and because she had bottled it up for so long. By having the strength to be open about what she was experiencing, she gave me the opportunity to help her work through the excess emotions and provide her with some coping strategies she could use both before and during competition. Madison ended up playing extremely well and was a key part of helping the team earn its way into the finals.

People are often under the mistaken impression that it shows weakness to admit they are struggling, but in fact it's the opposite; it shows strength. It's harder to face the truth sometimes, but it's the path to achieving better outcomes and living a more successful and fulfilling life.

High-Performing Minds are honest about their deficiencies and struggles, but they place a greater priority on self-improvement. By being open and honest with ourselves about our weaknesses and areas that need change or improvement, we exponentially accelerate our progress toward our goals.

This brings us to the end of the fourth segment on our path to a High-Performing Mind.

The next segment on our path up the hill to a High-Performing Mind is to learn how to manage through the adversity that can come from other people's comments and opinions. We'll want to strengthen our resilience and emotional armor so we don't get knocked off course on the way to achieving our goals. Let's find out what we can do next in Chapter 5.

Summary of Tools:

Tool #1: Acknowledge Your Weaknesses & Needed Changes

Tool #2: Prioritize Self-Development Over Denying Flaws

Let's Make This Stick

1. Identify an area of your life where you would benefit by acknowledging and making a needed change.

---

2. Identify a specific weakness that you would like to improve.

---

3. List three actions you can take to improve this weakness.

i. _____

ii. _____

iii. _____

4. Describe how your life would improve if you made these changes.

_____

_____

_____

_____

_____

_____

CHAPTER 5

Sticks & Stones May Break My Bones
But Painful Words Can Strengthen Me

I worked for many years in hospitality. One well-known characteristic of the industry is that while most customers are happy and appreciative of their hospitality experiences, this isn't always the norm. Inevitably, at some point, someone would let you know—and not always in the most pleasant way— when an experience they were hoping for didn't meet expectations. Or better yet, how you personally may have fallen short.

I remember one such occasion, many years back, at the beginning of my career at an affluent country club I worked at. Two members of the club—the parents of a tween who participated in a kid's sports program I developed and coached—criticized how we were doing things. They let me know directly and with an unexpected "assertiveness," that they weren't happy with the program or my performance. And even worse in my books, they requested a meeting with my boss and me to discuss their concerns.

This was a near-worst-case scenario in my mind. First, I prided myself on the quality and success of the program I had created. Second, this was the first complaint about it or me personally. And third, even though I had heard countless rave reviews from others about the program, the negative feedback and personal criticism stung, and it stung deeply.

My good ole self-defense mechanism didn't waste any time getting involved. "Stupid members," I thought to myself. "What do they know about programs anyway," was the opening salvo. It didn't stop there… "That kid of theirs has always been the problem." "Everyone knows they're difficult members, so no surprise they complained."

Noticing that I was getting myself worked up, I resolved to put it out of my head, took a few deep breaths, and decided to not take it personally.

That lasted about twenty seconds. Self-defense was back but this time had brought his best friend—anger. "What's their problem and who do they think they are anyway? It's obvious their kid is the issue, and this clearly has nothing to do with me!"

Irritation—not about to be left out—jumped in too. "It's so frustrating that people like that are so unappreciative of my obviously outstanding efforts. Don't they know everyone else thinks the program is fantastic?" Eventually catching myself in the middle of another mental tirade, I resolved, once again, to put it out of my mind. *Okay, slow down; I'm not thinking about this anymore.*

Cue fear stage left; we all know he wasn't going to miss out on all the drama. "Oh no, what's my boss going to say? What if he believes them!"

My eyes went full saucer thinking of the ramifications. A sinking feeling crept into the pit of my stomach. *What am I going to do?*

This feedback loop continued. My emotions sloshed around from anger, irritation, fear, and everything in between—intermittently but relentlessly—for the remainder of the day. It was still on my mind that night when I went to bed. Every time I settled down and was about to fall asleep, I'd get myself all worked up again.

The pattern continued over the next few days—thankfully with a little less intensity—but still with an emotionally fueled persistence. The bottom line was that my feelings were hurt and I didn't feel the criticism was fair or justified. I knew I had always put in 100% effort to deliver the best programs possible. After giving it some more thought, I declared to myself that they were the problem, but for some reason though, this didn't seem to do much for my chafed emotions.

A couple of weeks passed before everyone could coordinate their schedules. The meeting with my boss and the disgruntled members couldn't have come soon enough as far as I was concerned. I was relieved I didn't have to wait any longer and could finally get it behind me. I was sure my boss would politely hear them out but then tell them how they had it wrong and promptly send them on their way. I expected no less.

When I entered the room where they were already sitting, I immediately stiffened up. My defense mechanism, which was back on high alert, was listening intently and ready to pounce.

The disgruntled members started the meeting by outlining their concerns in detail, but for some reason, my boss did not disagree. Also, as they went on, clearly exaggerating unjustified and made-up issues in my opinion, he didn't put them in their place once and didn't boot them out of the office at any point. I was indignant!

All my boss did was sit there, listen quietly, and note their issues. He finished up the meeting by telling them we'd do our best to make sure we addressed their concerns.

Self-defense was not happy! He was convinced this amounted to betrayal and was now in overdrive vilifying everyone. *I can't believe this; he seems to be agreeing with them!*

I swore they left the meeting looking smug and like they had won. On the other hand, I not only felt like I lost, but was feeling even more bothered about it than when I walked in. Brief fantasies of quitting my job and telling them all to shove it flashed through my mind. Fortunately, my common sense prevailed even though I wasn't happy. I did my best to look outwardly calm, despite broiling on the inside.

What I didn't realize then was that as a seasoned hospitality industry veteran, my boss was following "best-practices" in dealing with disgruntled customers. He sat there and listened quietly and patiently as they aired their grievances. He didn't take anything personally, which admittedly may have been easier since he wasn't emotionally involved, and never got defensive or tried to justify anything. Instead, he focused on what he thought we could improve on, thanked them for their "feedback," and assured them we would do everything we could to improve things going forward.

Once they were gone, he didn't take the time to reassure me that I hadn't done anything wrong or to not worry about what they said, which made me feel even more insecure. He also didn't reiterate that I was doing a great job with my program or that everyone else was happy with it. This was likely because he didn't think it was a big deal and was focused on solutions instead of my bruised ego.

Taking Things Personally

Once I had the situation behind me and the chance to reflect, I wasn't thrilled about how the meeting had gone. My pride was wounded and I was still defensive whenever I thought about it. I had clearly taken the whole thing personally.

The disgruntled parents had officially made my top 10 list of least-liked members, and similarly, my opinion of my boss dipped a little in the short term. All of this, as mentioned, was just a byproduct of having taken the situation personally and being defensive. None of these reactions were my fault. I couldn't help the way I responded; this was just how I naturally was at this stage in my life.

Tool #1: Don't Let People's Negative Words and Doubts Stop You Unnecessarily

Ultimately, I made the changes my boss suggested, and things went more smoothly, even if that family was always a bit disenchanted with me no matter what I did.

Thankfully, I didn't give in to my initial thoughts about quitting. I also didn't let their complaints curb my enthusiasm to deliver the best experience I could for the kids in my program.

This brings us to our **first tool** for this chapter: **Don't let people's words stop you unnecessarily.**

It's easy to let things get to you when you are sensitive by nature, which is how I was born. When I was a toddler, my parents nicknamed me "buckets," because if anyone said something unpleasant, admonished me, or if I got into trouble for something, my eyes would instantly fill with water. But somehow, miraculously, this was often as far as it went, and the tears only rarely poured out.

Fortunately, I grew out of my "buckets" faze, but being sensitive remained to a degree, though admittedly, it matured as I got older. I still felt things intensely but didn't take things as personally, so it evolved into a "superpower," of sorts. It helped make me more aware of people's feelings and emotional reactions to what I said. This has always been a big help in navigating through the nuances of people's behavior both at work and in my social life. I've also rarely had any ambiguity knowing how I felt about things.

So, while being sensitive can be a highly beneficial attribute, being oversensitive isn't desirable, nor is taking things personally or ruminating about a situation for weeks at a time. Nobody enjoys these, and such reactions can derail us emotionally, act as mental distractions, impact our self-esteem, and undermine our confidence in our ability to succeed.

None of these are attributes of a high-performing mind, nor conducive to achieving our goals, so it's important to make the most of these situations and *not* take them personally, if possible.

Fortunately, the incident with the disgruntled parents didn't impact my confidence in my ability to make the program successful like it could have.

Tool #2: Don't Take Things People Say or Do Personally

Working in an environment that exposed me to situations where I had to occasionally deal with disgruntled members enabled me to get a lot of "reps" in over the years.

Whether it was one of my co-workers, someone who reported to me, or me personally, there were plenty of opportunities to get better at dealing with conflict or harsh opinions. This was simply the nature of private country clubs. Members paid big fees, and as a result, had high expectations for the quality of service they should experience.

The giant hole that you could drive a truck through in my emotional armor that first time I got professionally criticized, got a little smaller from that initial experience—an unexpected benefit, even if I didn't enjoy the way it felt at the time.

Once we experience those first few negative interactions that criticize us in areas we are vulnerable, we start to see we can survive and recover from these—even if it doesn't feel that way at the time. We lived to tell the tale, so to speak, and while it hurt our hearts and bruised our pride, we eventually recovered. We know we are doing our best, so it isn't a reflection of not caring or not trying, but instead, just not being aware of how things could improve.

It's hard to notice this progression because it's so gradual. With each new difficult situation it hurts a little less and it takes a little more to get to us. The experience we get from going through similar situations also gives us perspective. We start to see patterns. We might observe some people not taking it personally when they get criticized, so we come see that it's possible to have other responses—higher-performing ones.

It's important to keep in mind that this process doesn't usually go in a straight line. Even after becoming more resilient in some areas of our lives, we are likely to still have holes in our armor in others. Some situations might also hit us much harder and penetrate more deeply than others.

This was certainly the case when it came to my performance in sports. Not long after university and near the time I decided to play squash professionally, I was blindsided by some insensitive comments from a friend's dad. He had a lot of opinions about what it took to be good at the sport, and I didn't seem to cut the mustard in his mind. He told me that I lacked the skill and talent I needed to excel.

The comment hurt and skewered my pride in an area that must have been very vulnerable. I believed his comments to the extent that for a several years I often felt self-conscious playing in front of people and feared they were judging my abilities negatively.

It also made me worry that I had limits on how good I could become because of worrying about this perceived lack of skill and talent. This fear haunted me for a long time, reducing my enjoyment of the sport, and filling my body with tension when I competed and those doubts fluttered through my mind.

While this vulnerable area may have been a doozy, again, slowly over time, I became more resilient to comments of this nature. Eventually, even if it was at a glacial pace, I got to the point where it really didn't matter what anyone said; I was going to prove to myself, and anyone else who cared, that I could do it.

This brings us to our **second tool** for this chapter: **Don't take things people say or do personally.**

From Thin to Thick Skinned

Thanks to experiences like these over the years that challenged my insecurities, I developed thicker skin and improved at no longer taking things personally. If I made a mistake, I'd genuinely have no issue owning it and sincerely apologizing. I knew I was aiming to do my best at all times, had good intentions, and wanted to improve, so was open to their observations. Once I sifted through the unpleasant manner in which an unhappy customer or upset person might deliver their feedback, I zeroed in on what they were trying to say. I then assessed whether it was something I could help with to improve their experience or if they were just blowing off steam because they were having a bad day.

For example, a few years back, someone close to me told me they thought an important project I was working on would fail and that I lacked the reputation and social standing to make it a success. I felt genuinely concerned initially and listened closely to what she had to say—in case there was anything of value I could use later because I cared about her opinions, which were often helpful.

I acknowledged there was always a chance my plan wouldn't work, but I wasn't bothered by that possibility at that moment in time. I had a clear vision of what I was doing and why I was doing it. I could see that her negative opinions masked her own worries and fears, so I didn't take them personally. Her thoughts on my chances for success didn't deter me. If anything, her comments showed me some potential problem areas to keep an eye on to give myself the best chances to achieve my goals. Her comments also inspired me to finish the project and prove what could be possible.

After many years of working in hospitality, I even found some of the excessively negative comments entertaining—because of how absurd they could sometimes be. It's just a by-product of having worked in the industry for so long and hearing so many complaints. Some complaints are, of course, legitimate, but many are also trivial in the grand scheme of things. It's all a matter of perspective.

Eventually, as I learned to keep myself open to the emotional pain and discomfort, as mentioned earlier, I took things less personally. This didn't mean that things never bothered me. Occasionally, I would still get an initial twinge or two when something unusual came along, but it quickly passed. I would then move on to listening and seeing if anything could be improved—much like my boss did back when those disgruntled parents complained about my program.

This strengthening of emotional resilience can be observed when watching the evolution of an athlete who competes. When kids first start playing sports, they tend to wear their emotional highs and lows on their sleeves. When something doesn't go their way, or they make a mistake, or their opponent starts winning, you can visibly see the disappointment and sense of dejection on their faces and in their body language. This can last for large periods of time, sometimes an entire game, and impact their performance as they mope around the field or court feeling upset.

As kids get older, these "down" periods don't last as long. They move on and re-engage more quickly and fully, using 100% of their mental and emotional resources to play at their best. Hence, they start to optimize their performance to get better overall results.

For those who reach the expert or professional level, they have re-engaged so quickly after a disappointing moment that you hardly notice any deviation. They immediately return to being 100% fully engaged and don't spend valuable moments dwelling on the past. They are present in the moment and focused on what they are trying to achieve. More on this in Chapter 11.

Tool #3: Remember, Hurtful Words Can Strengthen Us

Things that challenge us make us stronger, which brings us to our **third and final tool** for this chapter. While sticks and stones can break our bones, **remember, hurtful words can also strengthen us**—if we are open to this possibility.

There is no denying that people's words can hurt. But by willingly going through the emotional pain and continuing forward, we strengthen our ability to handle and manage these situations. By changing our attitude about people's hurtful words and seeing them as opportunities to get stronger and grow, instead of only negative situations we shouldn't have to experience, we will benefit in the long run.

As time passes, we will learn to recover more quickly so that we can continue toward our goals with as little delay as possible.

High-performing minds don't let other people's negative words and doubts deflate their enthusiasm to achieve their goals and live their best life.

Three Tools to Strengthen our Emotional Armor:

Tool #1: Don't let people's words stop you unnecessarily
Tool #2: Don't take things people say and do personally
Tool #3: Remember, hurtful words can strengthen us

Congratulations, you've made it past the first section of *A High-Performing Mind, which is a major milestone* on your path up our hill to having a High-Performing Mind! Let's take a moment to look back on what we've covered and how far we've already come.

You started by establishing your primary desire, increasing your self-discipline, and the power of your personal will. Then by preparing mentally— that it won't always be easy to achieve your goals and to expect this, you've become more resilient. This will help to ensure that you persevere through any adversity and setbacks that come your way.

In addition, you've committed to always giving your best effort and you are now accelerating toward your goals by being open about what you need to improve or change to get there. Finally, you are now developing some strong emotional armor so that other people can't knock you down on your climb to achieving your goals and building your optimal life.

In the next section, Training the Mind, we'll find ways to help you make the most of your failures and mistakes and ensure you are thinking about the process and not merely the outcomes. We'll then harness the power of patience and self-restraint—to keep your mind resilient and focused while aiming to achieve your goals. From there, we'll cover how to get unstuck when everything seems negative and bleak. Finally, we'll move on to overcoming fear and figuring out how to bring the empowering state of flow and some extra courage into your daily life so that you can find your best performances and results when it matters most.

Let's Make This Stick

1. Give an example of the first time you remember feeling really wounded or hurt after being criticized by someone for something and write it down:

_____

1b. Did you learn anything from this situation? Did you receive any feedback that led to any changes either willingly or grudgingly?

---

2. Can you think of an example of something you used to take personally, bot no longer affects you with the same intensity?

---

3. List some hurtful words you've recently heard that were directed toward you. Is there any positive way you can use these words to improve your life and if so how?

PART II

— THE MAIN FLOOR —

TRAINING THE MIND

CHAPTER 6

What Else Do You Really Want?

Creating Your Master Plan

In chapter one, you identified your primary desire, and you started working on it right away by using our second tool—self-discipline. With your primary desire established, it's time to drill down a little further and add some additional goals to power you forward.

Let's start with an all-important question: If you could make a wish list of anything you wanted, what would be on it? Before you write anything down, let's first clarify exactly what *type* of want we're looking to add to this list.

Wants come in all kinds of shapes and sizes. I've personally wanted a variety of things over the years. When I was a kid, I wanted my parents' affection, I wanted to watch TV, I wanted candy, toys, a dog, a bike, friends, and at one point, I even wanted a little sister.

I told my mom about this specific request one day after she told me she was expecting. Instead, a few months later, I got another brother. Hadn't I clearly ordered a sister? Six-year-old me didn't get it. Luckily, it ended up working out with this unexpected brother. Fast-forward several decades and we're still best friends.

Beyond wanting a sister, I also wanted to do well in school and be good at sports. Truth be told, I actually wanted to be the smartest in my class and the best on any team I played for. Was this realistic? Probably not, but I was a kid and never told anyone my goals, so nobody ever told me it wasn't possible.

When I was about fourteen years old, I got invited to go on a trip to Hawaii with my friend Darren and his family. I couldn't wait to try surfing when I got there. I remember arriving at the beach the first day and running over to rent a surfboard.

With no concept that it wouldn't be as easy as the pros made it look, Darren and I ran out into the water and got started. There were four-year-olds and dogs going by on surfboards; how hard could it be? After an hour or two of repeated slips, falls, and chafing so bad I thought my nipples were on fire, we found out. It turns out surfing is pretty damn hard! I promptly returned the board and was crystal clear that I *never* wanted to surf again!

When I turned seventeen, I wanted a car and got one. Then I decided I really wanted a girlfriend. Unsurprisingly, the girlfriend idea soon supplanted all my other goals and occupied my mind for large portions of most days. Once I finally met someone special—which took quite a while—my focus moved on to getting into a university, getting good grades and making the school team.

Over the course of my life since my college days, I've also wanted jobs, loyal friends, to get married, have kids, excel in my careers, contribute positively to the planet and be helpful to others. What I've wanted has naturally evolved and changed over the years. The one thing these different periods of my life all had in common was that there has always been something I wanted.

Short-Term Wants vs. Goals

If we look back over my list of wants above, it becomes apparent that it can be divided into two broad categories. The first type of want is short-term in nature and won't necessarily need us to change to make these a reality. Short-term wants don't typically take a long time to achieve and can include buying something or going somewhere. We make the decision, maybe save a little money, and eventually go out and do it. We aren't generally required to make any significant changes to achieve a short-term want.

The second category of wants is what this chapter is all about and can be defined as goals. These are generally longer-term in nature and involve achieving something. Goals can require us to go through a step-by-step *process* to change ourselves for the better in some way.

Getting fit, doing well on a presentation, wanting to make more money, improving our health, mastering a craft, excelling in a career, completing a degree, winning a championship, and finding a life partner are all examples of goals. These usually require sustained effort and there's plenty of time for mistakes, setbacks, and failures along the way.

Goals can require consistent daily time and effort to build something, learn something new, or improve ourselves in some way—like strengthening our bodies or minds—or change the way we do things. They can require us to develop new or existing skills and to find a way to perform more proficiently in our pursuits.

Getting Real About What We Really Want

Our first task in developing our goals, as mentioned at the beginning of this chapter, is to get extremely clear and focused about what we want to achieve in our lives. We will do this by going through five quick and easy steps to develop a *Master List of goals* to ensure we have everything we'll need to live the fulfilling life we are hoping for.

The first thing we can do for ourselves when we start coming up with our Master List of goals is to be completely honest about what we want. This may sound easier than it actually is because notions about what we think we *should* want, or what we think others want for us, can interfere and sneak their way onto our lists.

If we want a happy, fulfilled life, it's important to be as honest as possible about what we really want deep down inside and not be influenced by what others might think.

In other words, what do you wish for when you blow out the candles on a birthday cake, find a four-leaf clover, or daydream about having or experiencing in your life?

Step 1: Create Your List of Goals

Now that you're starting to get clear about what you want, you're ready to take the **next step** of your climb up the hill to a High-Performing Mind: **create your list of goals.** Go ahead now. Grab a piece of paper (or use the designated pages at the end of this chapter) and write down anything that comes to mind. Try using the following list of questions if you need a little inspiration:

What are some things you want to experience?

What are some things you want to do?

Is there work that inspires you?

What adventures do you want to go on?

Are there things you want to achieve?

What things do you want to see happen in your life?

How do you want to feel?

What excites you?

What's important to you?

What will help you feel good about who you are?

Who do you want to be for yourself and to those around you?

Hopefully these questions spur some creative ideas.

As you identify your goals and write them down, it's important to make sure you leave them somewhere you will see them on a regular basis. Once you've gone through all the steps, put your list on a wall, or a door, or the top of a computer screen—anywhere that stands out and will catch your eye on a daily basis. This is a powerful way to stay clear and focused on what's important and what you're trying to achieve. It also helps you avoid unnecessary distractions.

Step 2: Reframe What You Want into Positively Stated Goals

Now that you have your preliminary list of goals, you'll need to take a few more simple steps to exponentially increase their effectiveness and your chances of making them a reality. This includes the **second step, reframe what you want into positively stated goals.**

When my son Jack was ten years old, he told me one day that he was feeling down about something. We chatted a bit and he confessed he was worried about how he was doing in school and said, "I really don't want to fail and get bad marks."

I listened and then asked, "Yeah, but then what do you want?"

He glanced at me with a confused look on his face like "Umm, didn't you just hear me?" He then repeated more patiently than I would have had our roles been reversed, "I don't want to fail at school and get bad marks…at school."

"I get that," I told him. "But that's what you *don't want*. What exactly is it that you'd like to see happen?"

He paused, not sure what I meant.

"Well, you said you don't want to fail at school, what's the opposite of that?" I asked.

He hesitated for a few seconds before catching on. "I want to pass and get good marks?"

"Yes, perfect," I said. "And what exactly would that look like?"

It took a little prompting, but he eventually got to the point where he said, "I want to do well in all my subjects and improve my grades to B's or better."

It was a simple change but an empowering one. Instead of Jack worrying constantly about what he was afraid *might* happen, he developed a clear picture of what he wanted and what he would have to do to get the outcome he was looking for.

This is how we reframe our goals into the positive.

Transform Negatives into Positives

The first thing I do when someone is looking for help with something is to ask them exactly what they want in the situation. I'll usually clarify by asking follow-up questions, like I did with Jack, until we get what they want framed into a positive, actionable statement. The reason for this is to get our energy and actions focused on the outcomes we want, rather than the situations we're trying to avoid.

"What do you want?" This may sound like a simple question and sometimes it is and we know the answer right away:

"I want to do well in school."
"I want to ace this presentation."
"I want to have a good relationship with my partner."
"I want to lose some excess weight."
"I want to eat healthier."
"I want to play better golf."

These are all examples of positively stated goals.

Sometimes though, it's not so clear what we want, but we're very sure about what we'd like to avoid, like my son Jack was.

"I don't want to get bad marks."
"I never want to be unprepared again."
"I don't want to fail my exam."
"I don't want to end up without any friends."
"I don't want to be so out of shape."
"I don't want to keep losing all the time."
"I don't want to get fired."
"I never want to feel that way again."
These are all examples of negatively stated goals.

Stay Focused on What We Want Instead of Don't Want

I worked for years with a maintenance worker named Carlo who was obsessed about the possibility of losing his job. He'd literally ask me at least once a week, "Hey Andrew, have you heard anyone say anything bad about me or my work? Do you think they'll fire me?"

It didn't matter how often I reassured him or suggested things he could do to ensure people were happy with his performance at work, it never seemed to help. He stayed firmly fixated on his greatest fear: getting fired.

Sure enough, even though it took over twenty years, the day finally arrived and poor Carlo got fired for not doing his job well.

I guess there's something to be said about self-fulfilling prophecies. Clearly Carlo would have been better off spending his time taking concrete actions to improve his performance instead of wasting his energy gossiping with people and trying to gauge their opinions on the chances he would keep his job.

We start emulating the way a High-Performing Mind thinks by reframing our negatively stated goals into positively stated goals. When the negative version of what we want is the first thing to come to mind, then we'll be better served to reframe it into the positive. For example, "I never want to be unprepared again," becomes "I want to ensure I'm always fully prepared." Continuing in this vein, a positive version of "I don't want to fail my exam," would be "I want to get a good grade on my exam." "I don't want to end up without any friends," could be restated as "I want to have several good friendships." "I don't want to fail in my marriage," would become "I want to succeed in my marriage." "I don't want to be so out of shape" would be positively framed as "I want to get into good shape," and "I don't want to get fired," would be more effectively focused on with what we want to achieve: "I want to excel at my job."

Let's quickly tackle any negatively stated goals we may have on our lists now by reframing them into positively stated goals as per above. Go through your lists now and circle any goals that start with "I never," I don't," etc. Rewrite each circled one now as a positively stated goal and cross the old negative versions off your list.

Done? If so, you've officially acquired a new skill. Once you've completed this step, you can now say you are able to transform negatives into positives.

Step 3: Get Clear and Specific About What You Want

Once we have reframed our goals into the positive, **our third step** is to get **clear** and **specific**. What exactly do we need to *do* to achieve our goals and overall vision of success?

We now take each of the positively stated goals on our list and elaborate on them to make sure they are both clear and specific. For example, "I want to do well in school," could be expanded to "I want to maintain a GPA of 3.5 or above in all my courses this semester." In this case, we're spelling out exactly what "doing well" would mean and what specific result we're looking for.

Similarly, we would need to drill down further into a goal like "I want to ace my presentation." What would this look like? Our second attempt might end up as, "I want to communicate my four main ideas, speak passionately about my topic, and know my material thoroughly so I can answer any question from the audience."

Continuing through our list of goals, "I want to get into shape," would be clearer and more specific as, "I want to lose ten pounds of fat and gain five pounds of muscle by the end of the year." Finally, "I want to excel at my job," could be restated as "I want to efficiently complete all my tasks before deadlines, produce high-quality work, and get along well with team members."

Take a moment now to expand upon each of the positively stated goals you have already written down and ensure they are all also *clear* and *specific*.

Step 4: What Are You Going to Do About It?

Now that we have some positively stated goals that are both specific and clear, our fourth step is to dive into exactly what we're going to do about it? We need some concrete *things that we will do* to make our goals a reality. In other words, your goals need actions!

Getting back to the story about my son Jack from earlier in the chapter. The next thing I asked him, once he had clearly stated that he wanted to pass all his subjects and improve his grades to Bs or better was, "Okay, so what are you going to do about it?"

With some extended discussion on what was reasonable for him to do to make his goals a reality, we came up with a list. He would get up early each morning to work on his math. He would start doing one hour of homework daily after school instead of his current once a week approach. He also agreed he would tell my wife and I about anything he didn't understand in class, so we could help him when we got home from work that evening. Lastly, he promised to write more thorough answers on tests in lieu of the one-liners he had been doing to that point—which were getting him only partial marks.

It was a solid plan and slowly over time, he started to turn things around and feel happier about his performance in school.

Our goals are only a dream until decisive actions are taken to make them a reality. What are the first steps and actions you will take?

Listing at least one action you will *do* for each goal is a good place to start. Write down each action underneath each of your goals now.

Step 5: The "Yeah, But How Much Do You Want It?" Test

We've come a long way, but there is one more important thing to find out: how much do we want each of our goals? Our fifth (and final) step in this chapter of our climb up the hill to a High-Performing Mind, is to review our list of goals and to do a desire test. We need to have strong emotion behind each of our goals or we won't get far.

It's important to mention at this point that yes, it's extremely helpful to write down clear and positively stated goals and actions on how we'll achieve them. *But* they won't have much value if there isn't strong *DESIRE* behind them. In other words, making sure we really want each goal will provide us with the high-octane motivation and passion needed to follow through and do what we said we would in order to make them happen. So, it's gut check time. After reading each one, ask yourself, "Yeah, but how much do I want this?"

At this point we're looking for a visceral emotional response:

- Is this goal important to you?

- Can you emotionally feel how much you want your goal to become a reality?
- Where in your body do you feel it? Does it make you feel energized?
- Are you willing to do whatever it takes to make it happen, even if it means persevering through difficult periods where you might feel like giving up?

If you can answer *YES* to these questions and feel how much you want your goals to become a reality, then you're well on your way!

Your Master List of Goals = Your Life Vision

Let's quickly recap everything you've done so far in this chapter. You now have a Master List of Goals that are positively stated, clear, and specific and that have concrete actions tied to them. You also have strong desire for each of them to happen. This is everything you'll need to begin and by creating this list, you're already on your way.

All the positively stated and specific goals you have written down now collectively start to become your *vision* for your life. You know what you want, where you are going, and what you need to do to get there. Most importantly, you have also packed enough fuel—in the form of strong desire—to ensure you don't run out of energy before you succeed.

Now that you have more clarity about your goals and the things that matter most to you, along with the foundational skills and abilities from the first section of the book, you are prepared and ready to tackle some of the other obstacles that can block you from achieving your goals. Chapter 7 will help us ensure we don't quit prematurely if we fail or experience setbacks. We'll also need to ensure we make the most of these moments to learn from our mistakes so that we can make adjustments and figure out our next steps forward. Let's keep going!

Let's Make This Stick

1. Write down your list of goals:

What are some things you want? What are some things you want to do or experience? Is there work that inspires you? What adventures do you want to go on? Are there things you want to achieve or accomplish? What things do you want to see happen in your life? How do you want to feel? What excites you? What's important to you? What will help you feel good about who you are? What kind of person do you want to be both for yourself and to those around you? Write them down now:

_____

_____

_____

2. Write down three positively framed goals that matter to you:

---

3. Rewrite each of these goals so they are *clear* and *specific*. Spell out exactly what needs to happen to achieve each goal:

---

4. Write down three concrete actions you will take to achieve each of these clear and specific goals from Question 3:

---

5. List your positively reframed, clear, and specific goals, and actions here to make your Master List. Perform the "Yeah, but how much do you want it," test on each one. Remove any that don't pass this test and replace them with one of your other goals that do.

_____

_____

_____

Congratulations, you have just accomplished something important on your road to strengthening your mind and empowering your determination. You now have your Master List of goals and can start realizing your VISION for what your optimal life looks like, another important milestone!

CHAPTER 7

Explore, Experiment, and Fail Your Way to Excellence

Learning from Our Setbacks and Failures

When I was about seven years old, my friend JJ and I decided it would be fun to ride our bikes down a large hill at a park not far from where we both lived. Seizing the moment, we grabbed our bikes and headed over before our parents could catch on to our plan.

When we arrived, we pushed our bikes up some winding paths to the top. As we stood there and looked down "Dead Man's Cliff" as it was known around the neighborhood—which surprisingly wasn't the slightest deterrent for either of us—we came up with our plan. I would go first (clearly, he was smarter than I was), put my brakes on the moment I crested the hill, and hold them the entire way down if necessary—so I didn't go too fast of course.

Sound reasoning, my brain told me. JJ agreed wholeheartedly, "Good idea, that way nothing can go wrong."

Peering over the edge of this steep and dried out old hill, I felt 100% confident I would make it down without any issues, and my thoughts agreed whole-heartedly, *This is going to be amazing!* With a brief nod toward JJ and barely the tiniest hesitation, I pushed off.

Things went really well for the first one to two seconds, but I then started accelerating at an exponential rate.

By mid-way down, I knew I was in trouble. Frantically stomping on the brakes as planned, did nothing to slow me down, and the landscape was now whipping by at what felt like a hundred miles an hour!

Before I had time to come up with a plan B, and maybe bail, I hit the bottom of the hill, which unexpectedly curved upwards. I launched into the air, over rotating upside down for about fifteen feet before landing unceremoniously on my head.

JJ slid down to make sure I wasn't dead. Luckily, all I had was a giant goose-egg on my head to remind me of the ill-advised series of decisions I had just made. "Stupid plan!" I glared at JJ, like it was somehow all his fault.

Annoyed, I dragged my bent-up bike back home and contemplated how I would explain this one to my parents.

Mistakes = Learning Opportunities

Clearly, seven-year-old me made a few miscalculations while contemplating my chances of getting down "Deadman's Cliff" safely. I just figured it would go well. From my limited life experience at the time, brakes had always made things stop without fail. Surely they would work on a 60-degree decline too?! Evidently not, as I quickly learned.

It was my first major life failure, and a broken bike and a sore head were reminders of the poor choices I had made. On the bright side, though, I learned a few valuable life lessons: Every situation is unique, it hurts to land on your head, and gravity should always be respected Oh, and more importantly, don't ever trust JJ again!

Obviously, it wasn't as fun as I hoped, but the bottom line is that in every failure, there's the potential to learn—if we're open to change and looking for it.

Let's explore a little further.

After college, Nigel, an entrepreneurial friend of mine, founded his first start-up, which grew quickly into a financial success. Not long after, he developed another new idea for a related business. He needed to finance it, so a colleague connected him to a wealthy investor to pitch his idea.

The day of the meeting, he went in confident, knowing he had a proven track record and a strong case for the new business. He delivered what he thought was a good presentation that demonstrated his concept and the financial viability of his plan. The investor, an older gentleman, leaned back in his chair and seemed to be listening attentively the whole time but said nothing when he finished.

Nigel waited a bit, and then asked if he had any questions. The investor leaned forward, clasped his hands together on the desk in front of him and said, "Yes, I do."

He first told Nigel he thought his idea was interesting. Then he asked, "But have you ever failed?"

Surprised by the question, Nigel replied, "What do you mean?"

The investor looked at him intently and repeated, "Have you ever failed?"

Nigel thought about it. He had always done well in school and his first business was a success, so he answered honestly, "No, I've never failed."

Nigel relaxed a little after giving his answer, figuring it had cemented the deal and ensured him the financial backing he was hoping for. The investor leaned back in his chair again, looked him in the eye and said, "Well, come back when you have," and then got up and left the room.

Nigel was shocked. The meeting didn't end at all the way he was expecting. Ultimately, he moved on and launched the second company, which ended up doing well.

I only heard this story from Nigel long after it happened, but he admitted the investor's question had caught him so off-guard that he still thought about it from time to time, even though it happened over twenty years ago.

While we can't know for sure what the investor was looking for in that particular meeting, it does make you wonder why anyone would want an individual who's failed to lead their company?

We can probably say with a high degree of probability that the investor wasn't looking for someone who was prone to making mistakes or poor judgments. What value is there then in having failed? And how does failure improve what we bring to the equation?

We can gain some insight into what our investor might have been looking for in Nigel and what he felt he lacked by exploring **our three mental tools for this chapter:**

Tool #1: Losing is learning - make the most of losses and failures

Tool #2: Explore, experiment and fail your way to mastery

Tool #3: Remember mistakes can make us more valuable not less

Tool #1: Losing is Learning- Make the Most of Losses and Failures

The first time I failed in a big way in school, was in a grade nine typing class. I was an over-confident teenager who spent more time socializing in class instead of paying attention and working hard. I had usually gotten decent marks up to that point, so thought I was getting away with it. My typing teacher, Mr. Babcock, however, was showing signs he wasn't seeing things the same way.

Babcock wasn't impressed that I didn't seem to be taking his class seriously and kept handing my assignments in late. He warned me repeatedly he would stop giving me chances, but he didn't seem to follow through, so I wasn't too worried about it.

At the end of the term, we had one big final assignment due, which was worth 50% of our grade. Of course, procrastinating and fooling around as usual, I did it, but I handed it in a couple of days late. Typing was just an afterthought in my mind. The easiest course I could take in high school I figured.

I didn't give it a second thought until my mid-year report card arrived. I scanned it quickly to check my overall average for the term and noticed it was much lower than usual. I had somehow missed the honor roll, which I was sure I was on track for. I couldn't figure out how my GPA had dropped so much? *There must be some kind of mistake!*

I slowed down and looked at each mark individually. My eyes bulged as they locked in on a big red 40% next to typing class. *40% in TYPING?* I couldn't believe what I was seeing. The only thing that made sense was that Babcock hadn't counted my final assignment. An awful sinking feeling crept into the pit of my stomach; this was going to be another tough one to explain to my parents.

Though it didn't feel that way at the time, Mr. Babcock did me a favor by holding me accountable. The result of this first big failure was some humbling for an overconfident kid who didn't recognize there were consequences for missing deadlines in the real world.

Fortunately, the experience of failing typing class taught me a bunch of important lessons I would later draw from in multiple areas of my life:

- It helped me appreciate how I shouldn't take things for granted.
- It pointed out that I needed to take responsibility for my actions.
- It showed me what poor judgment looked like and how that could play out.
- It also taught me a little humility for good measure.

This is a simple example of the positives that can come out of failing. Fortunately, I made the most of this setback and took things much more seriously at school, making sure I thought long and hard about missing any deadlines in the future!

The lessons learned from this one failure gives us insight into why Nigel's prospective investor would have increased interest in partnering with someone who had failed before. Who wouldn't prefer to work with someone who was more accountable, had a keener grasp of consequences, and exercised better judgment than they did previously? These qualities certainly point to higher performance in the future.

But what else? Is there anything more that failing does for us? Let's borrow a lesson from the world of sport to explore a little further.

Losing Is Learning

The ramifications of winning and losing are deeply ingrained in competitive sport, so athletes know it's part of the deal when they sign up. Good coaches take advantage of losses and use them as "teachable moments" to help expand their student's understanding about what it takes to win. The line *"losing is learning"* is a favorite quote of mine and encapsulates this notion: In every loss or failure there's an opportunity to learn. The wisdom gained can pave the way for improvement, and ultimately, future success.

Anyone who's played a sport before can probably remember at least one moment when they felt like a failure. Those who are determined to succeed, find a way to persevere and learn from their setbacks. Failing at anything can hurt and be discouraging but has the potential to be the quickest way to improve. By figuring out what we need to do better next time, we're one step closer to achieving our goals. **What you learn in your hardest moment is the foundation for your best results.**

I coached a young athlete named Sean at an international event where he lost to someone he had a good chance of beating. Sean had started well, but he fell apart about half-way through, and things went down-hill quickly from there. After the loss, he felt dejected about his performance, knowing he could have done better.

Once Sean had some time to recover, I asked him three questions: "What worked? Where did things go wrong? What could you do to improve your performance in the future?"

We discussed it for a while and Sean concluded that the strategy he thought he needed to win didn't work, so he wouldn't use it the next time against this particular opponent. He agreed his lack of speed was a problem, so he planned to adapt his training to address this weakness. He also admitted to feeling discouraged mid-way through, which coincided with his performance suddenly getting worse. To address this mental lapse, we identified some coping strategies he could use to refocus on his game plan the next time he felt discouraged.

The defeat exposed Sean's lack of speed and coping abilities. Noticing first-hand how these specific things let him down provided Sean with the motivation to make changes to his approach.

This one failure gave him a lot of clarity on his shortcomings and what he could do to perform at a higher level in the future.

Being able to modify strategies that don't work, identifying weaknesses that need to be improved, and developing better coping skills, are invaluable lessons and widely applicable. This gives us some additional clarity on why a savvy investor might value someone who had some failures under their belt.

Tool #2: Explore, Experiment, and Fail Your Way to Mastery

This brings us to our **second tool- Explore, Experiment, and Fail Your Way to Mastery.** Exploring and experimenting with different ideas, strategies and methods is an important part of deepening our understanding of a subject and strengthening our capabilities.

Experimenting can be messy. We might put the wrong foot forward. But how else can we figure out how to progress beyond our current level of ability? Someone who has made mistakes knows what doesn't work, which would certainly be an attractive quality for the leader of a company you were planning to invest in.

A couple years back, I built an outdoor skating rink for the first time. Needless to say, mistakes were made. I did some research ahead of time, but it didn't cover every variable a person might encounter.

My backyard is narrow and uneven, so I had to improvise ways to close some gaps between the ground and the boards. I also thought making ice would be easy. Add water, combine with cold temperatures, *what could go wrong?* It turns out plenty of things.

The leaves and twigs sticking up out of cracked, uneven ice the first time the water froze were evidence of that.

As the season went on, I experimented with different ways to water the rink. I had to change my approach on warmer days, then change it again for exceptionally cold days. I slowly became more skilled at making ice you could actually skate on. Exploring different approaches, experimenting a little, and making some mistakes along the way helped me figure things out. Eventually, this made for a smoother experience for everyone who used the rink.

We see this in action when we watch kids play. You can almost hear them thinking, *What happens if I do it this way, or that way, or upside down, or hanging over this chair?* They naturally explore and experiment. They don't get concerned if something doesn't work. They just note it and keep going. It's no wonder kids who pursue something from a young age and stick with it can demonstrate a level of proficiency that far exceeds the adults who taught them in the first place.

Any time spent developing ourselves pays dividends down the road, like putting money in the bank. We may not always have the luxury of ideal practice methods and environments, but that should never stop us from experimenting. How much time we put into something is the key part of the equation, so if we can couple that with an intense desire to improve, we can find our way to the results we're looking for.

Ten Thousand Hours?

Ten thousand hours is commonly referenced as the measuring stick for mastery. It's a great reminder that it takes a significant amount of time and dedication to excel at a pursuit. I use a similar formula when speaking to anyone attempting to master a pursuit. *Volume X Talent = Greatness. Volume,* in this case, represents the amount of time spent practicing. *Talent* refers to a person's natural aptitude to improve from practice.

The second and more important part of the equation, is *Volume X Low Talent = Pretty Darn Good.* I always couple them together. Neither one is complete without the other:

Volume X Talent = Greatness
Volume X No talent = Pretty Darn Good!

These formulas used together illustrate that talent may be out of our hands, but volume isn't.

Perceived talent in kids in particular can change in directions we don't always anticipate as they grow and get older.

I have seen kids, who appeared steeped in natural talent at a young age become indistinguishable from their classmates by junior high. Conversely, I have observed young adults develop enormous physical and mental abilities that weren't there when they were kids.

Talent can manifest in ways that we don't always consider to be talent or in ways that are hard to see. Sometimes people possess a mental talent that gives them a vision to transcend what we would have thought them incapable of under normal circumstances.

Ice hockey legend Wayne Gretzky regularly finished last on his team in strength and fitness tests. He had the poorest peripheral vision on his team yet is the all-time greatest scorer his sport has ever known.

Albert Einstein began talking later than most toddlers and his teachers thought he was pretty average as a six-year-old in school, but he went on to be one of the greatest physicists of all time. People don't always measure up to traditional ideas of talent. If we're passionate about something and willing to put in the time and effort, we can't know how far we'll go. It's in our best interests to not rely on the assessments of others. We can only find our limits by trying for ourselves.

Optimal Practice Equals Optimal Results

From the perspective of those aiming to master something, there's more to the equation for high performance than putting in ten thousand hours of practice. The quality of practice is also an important part of mastering a pursuit. The expression, **optimal practice equals optimal results** gives us better insight into what it takes. If we were trying to improve our ability to shoot hoops in basketball, for example, technical flaws in our execution suggest we won't get very far, very quickly.

If we use the above "optimal practice" approach and include giving our best effort along with the willingness to explore, experiment, and fail to figure out our limits and weaknesses, we have everything we need to develop ourselves at warp speed.

If someone spends ten thousand hours practicing the same thing using a lazy effort level and sub-optimal approaches, they won't keep up with someone who spends the same amount of time practicing optimally. They'll improve faster again if they also explore and experiment along the way.

Tool #3: Mistakes Can Make Us More Valuable, Not Less

People seem to appreciate that excelling at something involves a lot of time, dedication, and learning. Despite this, there's a pervasive aversion to tolerating mistakes and failures from ourselves and others—two things that are inherent and integral to the learning process.

This aversion fundamentally contradicts strengthening our minds and becoming a high performer. If we accept that mistakes are a critical part of the learning curve, then why are we so condemning of others when they occur?

I remember conducting an interview for a junior coaching position. At one point we asked the candidate why he was no longer working at his last job. He paused for a moment, then went on to tell us about how he made an error in judgment and had a beer with a client on the premises, something which was frowned upon by his boss. They let him go not long after they found out.

Impressed by his honesty and integrity, and confident that he had learned a valuable lesson that day, we hired him. He ended up being a great coach and a fantastic member of our team. This interaction illustrates our **third tool: if we learn from mistakes, we become more valuable, not less.**

Harsh responses to errors can emphasize playing it safe and dissuade experimentation. But we need to experiment to reach a higher level of aptitude. Despite this, we are quick to punish or dismiss people for making errors when these very errors often make them better performers. From a team perspective, this punishment only shows everyone that mistakes will cost them, so it's best never to admit them. **You're the same person ten minutes after you fail, only wiser.**

If this is true, then why should we be afraid to admit our mistakes or be quick to judge others when they do? Context plays a big role with our perspective. If someone is generally a strong performer but makes an error in judgment, are they more or less valuable after that moment?

A friend told me a story about hiring a university graduate to help him with some trading in his investment company. "The kid" as he called him, had made a pretty colossal blunder on one of his trades not long after he was hired. So, I asked my friend if he fired him, and he replied, "Are you kidding me? It cost me $40k for him to learn that lesson. I'd be crazy to get rid of him now!"

His response made me laugh, but not because I thought he made the wrong decision. I admired how quickly he recognized and viewed "the kid's" mistake as the cost of some valuable training.

Not only is it in our best interest to learn from our own failures and mistakes, we can also benefit just as much when we allow others to do the same. They have the potential to learn and improve just as we do.

Taking ownership of our mistakes can be hard and bruise our ego. But it opens us up to learning and growth so we can become a high-performer in the future. **Creating an environment where people are afraid to explore, experiment, and make mistakes only dooms us to mediocrity.**

We can improve anything if we put in the time and effort. But like any process, we're going to make some wrong turns along the way. When you're feeling discouraged, remember that there's no greater teacher than failure: it ensures we have the lessons, the know-how, and the skills we need to reach that next level of excellence.

Let's Make This Stick

1. Give an example of a time when you experienced a significant failure:

_____

2. List at least three things you learned from that failure or how you're better from having gone through it:

i. _____

ii. _____

iii. _____

3. List three skills you would like to improve: ex. Ability to handle stress, leadership skills, parenting skills, ball control, drawing, patience, cooking, throwing, problem solving, etc. Be as specific as possible.

i. _____

ii. _____

iii. _____

4. List at least one thing you will do to improve each of the above mentioned skills: ex. Try some different strategies or approaches? Practice in a particular way? If someone wants to improve their patience, for example, they might practice consciously taking a deep breath in and out or counting to 3 before responding in stressful situations.

i. _____

ii. _____

iii. _____

CHAPTER 8

The Process Not the Outcome

Afterburners and the Power of Patience

Throughout my coaching career, I've been fortunate to work with some extraordinary human beings who have inspired me over the years. Though each has been unique in their own way, it has always amazed me how high performers share so many similar attributes and mental approaches as they push to achieve their goals. While some seem to possess these qualities innately, others appear to have picked them up along the way.

Nearly all of the high performers I've worked with openly pursued their passion and had an intense desire to excel and make it to the top of their chosen pursuits. They were all disciplined and unafraid to put in the necessary time and work to maximize their chances for success. Without exception, they devoted themselves completely to being the best they could be and achieving what they were aiming for.

These self-enhancing characteristics that these high performers shared also served them well in other areas of their lives. Doing their best was normal for them—as we talked about in Chapter

3—and they brought these habits into whatever pursuits that were important to them.

While high performers enjoy the benefits of having ideal mindsets already in place—something we can all strive toward and eventually achieve as well—it's important to note that they also experience personal challenges and struggles at times. Like the rest of us, they have to find their way through setbacks, failures, doubts, and fears.

I worked for many years with an impressive young athlete named Caitlyn, who was not only a star student who had graduated with a near-perfect GPA from her Ivy League school but somehow had also found the time to be one of the best players in her sport in the country.

From a young age, Caitlyn was someone who aimed extremely high yet, found a way to achieve nearly anything she set her mind to. More importantly though, what set Caitlyn apart in my eyes, was that to this day, she remains one of the hardest-working people I have ever known.

Caitlyn would attend classes, train several hours a day for her sport, go home, and then study until the early hours of the morning daily—and she did this for years. She did everything she could to finish all her assignments and make sure she was completely prepared for every exam and finish top in her class. At the same time, she also trained extremely hard to perform at her best and achieve her goals in her sport. She was humble, never spoke about all the hours she put in—unless directly asked about it—and never complained. Caitlyn was focused on what she wanted to do, and she exerted whatever effort she felt was necessary to give her the best chances of achieving her goals.

Despite this incredible mindset and desire to succeed, Caitlyn, like all of us, had to push through her own doubts, fears, and negative thinking. I had coached her for years, and she was always impressively positive and focused while competing. She rarely, if ever, wavered and was exceptionally consistent in her performance and results. On one occasion, though, I was coaching Caitlyn at the national championships for her sport, and she looked visibly upset and demoralized in a way I had not seen in the past. It was after losing the first set in the semifinals to someone she had never lost to before.

Caitlyn was the number-two-ranked player in the country at the time and was playing the third-ranked player, who had been nipping at her heels for years, but had always failed to get the better of Caitlyn. This time, though, things clearly were different.

It wasn't that Caitlyn wasn't playing well, but rather that her opponent started the match like a completely different player than either of us had come to expect. Caitlyn's opponent took a commanding lead from the beginning, dominated nearly every point, and won the first set convincingly. It was as if she had gone to another level and left Caitlyn behind. Caitlyn had been completely outclassed in every way.

Coming off the court during the break, Caitlyn looked shell-shocked and near tears, which was completely out of character for her. She told me she felt demoralized and couldn't understand what was going wrong. She felt like she couldn't win and had no idea what to do to turn it around. She was too focused on how well her opponent was playing and the newfound confidence she seemed to have.

We didn't have long to talk between sets, but I reminded Caitlyn to remember all the training and hard work she had put in over the last year and that she was ready for this challenge. I told her to keep trying and that she had to focus on her opponent's weaknesses, instead of how well she was playing. Caitlyn had to find a different way to win than she had in the past.

Caitlyn didn't look convinced as she went back on the court still looking dejected, but I hoped she had taken something from our conversation so she wouldn't give up prematurely and would keep searching for a way to succeed.

Fortunately for her, Caitlyn wasn't someone who gave up easily and she dug in extra hard during the second set. She was in survival mode. Although she fell behind early on, she turned on the afterburners and was able to battle back and draw even in the match through sheer determination and by dipping heavily into her fitness reserves. Even though it cost her physically, her approach worked. While she wasn't able to exploit her opponent tactically yet, Caitlyn muscled through and found a way to win the set and draw even.

Both players took turns taking the lead from there and the final set was a fierce battle. Caitlyn demonstrated she wasn't going down without a serious fight, and her opponent started to falter ever so slightly. This subtle emotional letdown by her opponent was enough for Caitlyn. Despite being completely exhausted, she was finally able to exploit some of her opponent's movement weaknesses—for an extremely hard-fought win.

After losing that first set despite playing well, Caitlyn had panicked. But she responded proactively when she needed to and was able to up her effort level, come back, and overcome a very tough opponent who was playing at her best. When all else had failed, Caitlyn fell back on her willingness to outwork anyone and give it everything she had to make it through.

While she didn't always succeed and did end up losing to a better opponent in the finals the next day, Caitlyn never let herself down from the perspective of always putting in the work and doing everything she could to maximize her chances of achieving her goals. Her sheer grit in the face of imminent defeat epitomizes our **first tool** in this chapter.

Tool #1: When All Else Fails, Use "The Afterburners" Before Giving Up

The value of this tool might be more apparent when it's considered in other areas of life outside of sports. Sometimes we just don't have any options, and giving it everything we have is the only viable way to move forward if we want to succeed. This can be true in our jobs or careers—for example, when a big project is due and we're running behind schedule. Our only option left, aside from failing and missing the deadline, may just be to give it our all and invest the time and energy necessary to get it done.

I remember having to produce a forty-page portfolio for an important job interview I had a while back. They gave us a narrow time frame to complete the work, but I felt confident that I was going to finish it well before the deadline. The night before it was due, though, I discovered a catastrophic formatting error that meant the portfolio would have looked terrible when it was viewed. This probably would have eliminated me from the next round of interviews in the highly competitive field of applicants. So, I did what I had to do. I stayed up until about 3AM, slept for two hours, and woke up to finish fixing it in time for the deadline the next morning. I ended up turning it in five minutes before it was due—a little too close for comfort!

The value of giving it everything we have before giving up can also be seen in our personal lives. When nothing else seems to be working to improve a relationship, if it's important to us, we can fall back on genuinely making the extra effort to improve things before moving on. Similarly, when experiencing a health crisis, we might have no other choice but to take extreme measures and do everything possible to improve our circumstances.

This was certainly the case for me with my health issues described in the introduction. Unless I was prepared to be permanently bedridden or worse, I had no other alternative than to try anything and everything I could think of to heal my body. I did it willingly and without hesitation since I just wasn't prepared to give up on myself or my family.

None of the above is to suggest that there aren't times and situations where it's wisest to move on. But when you aren't willing or able to do that yet, turn on those afterburners, give it everything you have, and go for it at least one more time. We often have more to give, even when we've hit what we think is our limit, and remembering this can help us dig a little deeper when we need it most.

Tool #2: Practice Patience & Self Regulation

Risky name for our **second tool** I know. I probably couldn't have chosen two less appealing terms and to make matters worse, I paired them together. Success, however, is rarely an overnight experience, and patience and self-regulation through the process of achieving our goals are often unrecognized superpowers in the equation.

My son Jack was a committed athlete from a young age. By the time he was ten years old, he played three sports at a competitive level. He had already identified the value of hard work and practice a couple of years prior, but when he turned ten, he started to make decisions—unprompted by either of his parents—that he felt would enhance his chances for success. It was nothing over the top, but it started with simple things like wanting to go to bed early before a big game or track meet and being interested in making healthy choices with his diet to maximize his energy during competition.

We also noticed it with his schoolwork. Jack liked to get his homework over with right away so he could enjoy the rest of his day without worrying about it. He started to recognize early on that by self-regulating a little here and there, he could enjoy things more when it mattered.

When I coached full-time many years back, I remember kids often complaining that practice was boring at times. "Too much repetition," they'd say. "We want to play more games!" And so on. One of my favorite responses to this was from one of the assistant coaches. He would look them square in the eye and simply ask, "Do you want to have fun now or when you win during competition?" This quickly silenced any debate, and it didn't take long for them to get back to doing those boring drills again.

As unappealing as patience may be, no honest conversation about achieving our goals would be complete without considering the power of patience and being able to wait for those first signs of success to finally crest the horizon. It can take some time for this to happen. Neither patience nor waiting screams fun but accepting them as part of the process of achieving success can help reduce premature concerns and unrealistic expectations as we strive to make our goals a reality.

Whatever long-term objective it is that you've set for yourself, it's going to take time and patience to achieve. And as is widely known, patience is a virtue that will serve you well. Big changes can be incremental and usually don't happen overnight. Building successful outcomes takes time.

One of my favorite examples of this is from the 2021 documentary, *7 Yards: The Chris Norton Story,* [a film] directed by Jonathon Link. Without giving away more than you can see in the trailer, it's an inspiring true story about Chris Norton who was tragically paralyzed after taking an unexpected hit during a high school football game. The film chronicles Norton's indomitable spirit as he takes this life altering-challenge head-on and goes about setting some extremely ambitious goals. He trains four to five hours a day to rehabilitate himself and achieve his dreams. His patience throughout his process and his determination to succeed are truly awe-inspiring. A little *patience* and *self-regulation* can go a long way.

Tool #3: Focus on the Process, Not the Outcome

Back when I was working my first full-time job as a squash coach after graduating from university, I remember walking by the reception area one day about three weeks after I started. I looked over and noticed one of the receptionists, who was standing behind the desk, waving an envelope in my general direction. "Your paycheck," she said. "Your paycheck is ready."

Paycheck?! The slow dawn of realization took a moment to register... *Oh yeah, I get paid for this!*

I was so busy building programs, coaching, and having fun doing it that I temporarily forgot they paid me to be there! But the joke was on them, as far as I was concerned, I would have done it all for free. Well not really, but that's how it felt at the time. Clearly, I was completely immersed in the process and not thinking at all about outcomes.

Being focused in the present moment helps exponentially improve performance and success in any endeavor. We'll explore this fully in Chapter 11. But it also keeps our minds zeroed in on the process, which is comprised of the things that are going to help us build our success. In my coaching work example above, the process included improving the programs and the quality of the instruction to elevate the experience for the club members. From a competing in the sport perspective, my process included all the practice and the training. When we focus on the process, the success takes care of itself.

None of this is to suggest that we shouldn't have a clear vision in our minds of what we want to achieve. But I'm highlighting that it's in the *doing* that we make it happen, not by just *thinking* about it or only imagining what it will be like when we finally get there. This is why our **third and final tool** for this chapter is to **focus on the process—not the outcome.**

Three Tools to Keep You Focused on Priorities and Doing Everything You Can to Succeed:

Tool #1: When all else fails, use the afterburners!

Tool #2: Practice patience and a little self-regulation

Tool #3: Focus on the process not the outcome

With Chapter 8 now under our belts, we've reached the ¾ point of our journey—another major milestone on your way to a High-Performing Mind.

The next section of our climb is figuring out how to get unstuck when negative thinking takes over and everything seems hopeless and bleak. We'll also improve our ability to find the positives amidst all the negatives when we get sucked into that quagmire of negative thinking. In the meantime, let's get out there and start doing!

Let's Make This Stick

1.Think of someone who inspires you. Write down their name and give at least one reason why you feel this way.

---

2. Take a moment to choose one thing in your life you would be willing to devote more hours to so you can increase your chances for success.

---

3. Identify one area of your life where it's time to go all in and give it everything you have.

_____

_____

_____

4. List one goal in your life that you need to exercise some patience and get more focused on the process instead of the outcome.

_____

_____

_____

5. What's one thing you can do today to increase your chances of achieving what's most important to you?

_____

_____

_____

_____

CHAPTER 9

Getting Unstuck

Finding the Positives in the Negatives

It's easy to get trapped into negative thinking spirals when things don't work out the way we hope. But if we work at it, as bleak as things can seam at times, it's possible to still find the positives in our negative moments. We can learn to make the most of our setbacks and failures.

I did some mental coaching work with a student named Sara who was in her first year of law school. She had just failed an important midterm and was feeling discouraged.

When we spoke that day, she told me her confidence had taken a hit after the exam and she was doubting her ability to succeed. She was feeling discouraged and overwhelmed with a slew of negative thoughts.

Sara described not being able to break out of her spiral of negative thinking. Doubts flew relentlessly through her mind: "I'm a failure, I can't do this, I'm not good enough, I'm never going to catch up, I hate myself for being in this situation, I don't want to experience this again," and so on. It was a mental whirlwind, and she felt trapped.

I listened carefully to everything Sara had said and started by asking her what her ideal vision was for herself in law school. In other words, what was her goal? She said that she wanted to master the material and be the top performing student in her class. Once Sara's goals were clear, I reminded her that there were positive things she could find in her negative experience of failing—if she looked for them.

We then zeroed in on a few specific negative thoughts that were bothering her the most. The goal was to help her find a better mental and emotional space so she could start taking concrete steps to achieve her vision of being the top student in her class.

"Which thought are you most worried about?" I asked her.

"The thought that I hate myself for being in this situation," Sara replied. "It makes me dislike myself and feel really discouraged about having failed."

The first thing I suggested was to acknowledge that any feelings of self-hate were misplaced. It was natural for Sara to feel disappointed in herself for having failed, yes. But what she hated was doing poorly on the midterm and not getting the results she was looking for, not herself. I then pointed out how this thought could be used to find some positive ways to respond and learn from the experience. Yes, she hated that she hadn't done well on the midterm, so what could she do about it?

Then I asked what concrete actions she could take to ensure she didn't repeat the same mistakes and find herself in the same situation again. Sara acknowledged that she hadn't put the time into learning the material thoroughly enough. She also told me she should have done three hours of study for every one hour of class time and had she done this, she would have done much better on the test.

Once she clarified the steps she could take, I suggested she write down her new three hours of study for each hour of class approach on a piece of paper and leave it somewhere she would see it daily. I suggested writing down, "I don't want to experience failing a midterm again, so I will study three hours a day for every one hour of class time to ensure I am prepared in the future."

By using her negative thoughts, "I hate myself for being in this situation," and "I don't want to experience this again," Sara was able to create a concrete plan with plenty of motivation for future success: "Ensure I am prepared by studying three hours a day for every one hour of class time."

We repeated this process again with her next most consuming thought: "I'm not good enough." We started by acknowledging that, in this situation, there was some accuracy to the thought; she hadn't prepared sufficiently to do "good enough" on the exam.

We then agreed that her first step for success—"Ensure I am prepared by studying three hours a day for every one hour of class time"—would help her do what she could to be "good enough" and prepared enough for future exams.

We then talked about Sara's negative thought: "I'm never going to catch up and do well in the future."

"Is there anything you can do to catch up?" I asked her.

She agreed there was and the three to one study to class time ratio would help.

Sara was able to use her negative thoughts to *map* her way back to her goal of being the top performing student in her law class. She transformed her negative downward spiral into upward momentum that empowered her toward the success she envisioned.

Getting Stuck on the Negatives

Getting stuck on negative reactions to our circumstances can happen to anyone at any time. I remember my parents telling me when I was a kid that they were going to take me to see *Star Wars*. I objected strongly, "No, not *Star Wars*, I don't want to see that movie!"

My parents were confused, but they persisted, "Don't worry, you'll love it, it's supposed to be fantastic."

I wasn't convinced. I definitely did *not* want to go. In the back of my five-year-old mind, I somehow thought *Star Wars* had something to do with the heavy metal band KISS. Bizarre, I know, but I can't for the life of me remember how I made this association other than a star shape, done in make-up, around one of the band member's eyes. I had seen them on TV and thought they looked scary. Since I wasn't a five-year-old head-banging, heavy metal fan, I obviously had no desire to see *Star Wars*. It may not have made any sense to anyone else, but it made perfect sense to me.

All I could think about leading up to the movie that day was how awful it was going to be. I continued to voice my objections as my parents pushed me out the door, into the car, and right up until we got into the theatre. Fortunately, they took it all in stride and weren't too concerned about the ramblings of their irrational kid. I walked in scowling, with my arms crossed and in a grouchy mood for being forced to go.

Well, needless to say, like millions of others, I ended up loving the movie and sat there completely enthralled. I came home exuberant about all the characters and wanted every *Star Wars* toy ever made from then on. It was a good thing my parents did some of my positive thinking for me and helped me get past the negative ideas I had about the movie.

Using Both Our Positive and Negative Thinking Abilities

Several years back I worked with an individual named Steve who also used to get stuck in negative thinking, but in his case it impacted him professionally. Steve was highly adept at identifying every problem that could arise with any of our project plans and new ideas. I looked forward to his perspective and found it valuable to hear.

Unfortunately, I also found that identifying the problems was usually where his feedback ended. I was hoping that Steve would offer possible solutions, workarounds, or at least some alternative ideas after identifying the areas of concern, instead of just a "nope, that won't work."

There's no doubt there is tremendous value in our ability to think negatively. It leads us to consider and eventually identify things that could go wrong ahead of time. It allows us to anticipate consequences, assess risk, and question whether or not we have all the resources we need to move forward and achieve our goals. If taken to excess, however, negative thinking can lead to inaction, diminished creativity, and a decreased rate of improvement, impairing our ability to reach our goals. Such was the case with Steve who took negative thinking to excess.

On the other hand, the benefits of positive thinking are more obvious and have been well documented. Positive thinking paints a picture in our minds about what we want or what could be and enables us to determine the benefits of doing something. It can inspire us, increase our confidence, and supply the energy we need to pursue the things we desire. It opens our minds to the world of possibilities and helps us find creative responses to our challenges and solutions for our problems.

A High-Performing Mind uses elements of both negative and positive thinking processes to achieve optimal performance. In addition, practicing getting ourselves "unstuck" when our negative thinking spirals will help us access our positive thinking abilities and stay on track toward our goals.

Finding The Positives in Our Negatives

As we know well by now, setbacks are part of the process of achieving our goals. The question is, how do we deal with them when they do come along? In earlier chapters, we covered how an ideal response to a setback is to learn from the experience, pick ourselves up, and continue toward our goals without much hesitation. Setbacks might also require making an adjustment or two to our approach (if needed) so we can find a better result the next time around.

Sometimes, however, the solution isn't clear. Feeling negative and discouraged about a failure can get the better of us and our confidence can take a hit, like it did for Sara. As we identified in my session with her that day, there are concrete steps you can take to pull yourself out of a negative spiral as quickly as possible. These steps involve finding the positives in the negative thoughts that are weighing us down. Let's go through each step in detail.

Step 1: Reaffirm Your Goal and Ideal Outcome

Imagine that you just experienced a major failure in an important area of your life and are feeling stuck in negative thoughts about what it means for you and your future.

The first step is to reaffirm what the ideal outcome would have been had you achieved your goal. For example, let's say you just did poorly in an interview. You say, "Okay, I just bombed that interview. Had I been successful the way I wanted; how would the interview have gone? What would my responses have been like, and how would I have felt at the end of it?"

As we saw in our opening story, after Sara's major setback, the first thing we did was get clear about her original goal and what it would look like if she achieved it. Clarifying her goal refocused her mind on what she wanted most in the situation, which then provided her with the energy and motivation she needed to get back on track.

Sara reaffirmed that her goal was to finish at the top of her law class. Ideally, any time she thought about this, it would give her the energy and motivation to follow through on what she needed to do to make this goal a reality.

Step 2: Identify The Negatives

When we're feeling particularly down after a setback, **the second step**, is to make a list of the negative thoughts, worries, and feelings that come to mind about the situation. In Sara's case, she had a bunch of negatives swirling around: "I'm a failure, I can't do this, I'm not good enough, I'm never going to catch up, I hate myself for being in this situation, I don't want to experience this again."

It's important to be open and honest about the negative sentiments you notice yourself thinking so you can write them down. Don't hold back. These negative thoughts will become your map back toward success.

Step 3: Take Positive Actions

Positive actions are far more powerful than negative thoughts. Our **third step** is to take our ideal vision from step one and identify some positive actions we can take to achieve it. For example, Sara's stated goal was to "finish top in her class." In order to achieve this, Sara decided that if she studied three hours for every one hour of class it would be a big step toward reaching her goal.

Sara only came up with one positive action toward her goal on this occasion, but there's no need to stop at one. Come up with as many actions as you want if it helps you turn things around and achieve your goals.

So, if your goal is to improve your health, what steps can you take right away to improve your chances? Can you make healthier eating choices to improve your diet? Could you find a way to exercise a little more? Is there a negative habit that is adversely affecting your health or well-being that you could reduce or stop?

List three positive actions you can take to improve your situation.

Maybe you're not getting the results that you want in a pursuit or at work and are feeling really negative and unhappy about it?

Again, take the time to sit down and list out the positive actions you can make to improve your circumstances. Do you need to devote more hours to succeed? Are there things you can reduce in other areas of your life to free up the extra needed time? Are there any negative habits that are holding you back? Let's find some positive changes and actions you can make and let's get to it!

Positive actions will always trump negative thoughts. When you find yourself struggling with negative thoughts, take positive actions to improve your situation. Doing this can quickly help us feel better about our circumstances.

Going through these three steps will help you get past the negative thoughts, doubts, and worries you get stuck on while trying to achieve your goals. By finding constructive ways to respond, you can let go of your negative emotional reactions, feel better with renewed purpose, and get back on track quickly.

Finding the Positives Through Difficult Times

Sometimes, we are challenged beyond our goals, and we have to find a way to stay positive during the most difficult of situations. We can get pulled down into despair as our world is upended by circumstances we could never have anticipated. Finding the positives in those profoundly negative and challenging periods can be exceptionally hard, but as we do, we can find our way through to happier times again.

This was certainly the case for my brother Aaron's young family.

When my nephew Easten was just 3 months old, he was diagnosed with an aggressive form of leukemia. It was an unexpected and devastating blow to our family, but especially for his parents: my brother and sister-in-law. We were all in utter disbelief that something like this could happen to someone so young and innocent.

The diagnosis turned their family's life upside down and split them in two. They each had to take extended turns at the hospital to care for their cancer-stricken newborn while the other was forty miles away, back home, keeping some semblance of their lives going and looking after Easten's three-year-old big brother.

It was an extraordinarily emotional and challenging time in their lives as Easten spent the next six months in the hospital, twice his short life span. Family, friends, and the local community didn't let them go through this terrible nightmare alone and stood firmly with them in an incredible display of love and support. They were brought food daily for months and toys for Easten as he underwent four rounds of chemotherapy and a stem cell transplant, which the doctors felt gave him his best chances for survival.

Easten was a year old by the time the weekly trips to the hospital finally abated. He had mostly known life to that point in his six by nine hospital room, but was finally able to get back to being a normal baby at home with his parents and big brother, who couldn't have been more excited to see him. They were together again under one roof, relieved to have this stressful nightmare behind them.

This joyful family reunion unfortunately lasted less than 18 months. Easten's cancer was back. The stem cell transplant had failed, and the leukemia was moving even more aggressively than it had the first time and was ravaging his little body.

Their world split into two once again as Mom and Dad took turns back at the hospital as he underwent another two rounds of chemotherapy, radiation, and a second stem cell transplant. To the relief of everyone, the treatments ended up doing the job and eliminating the leukemia from his two-and-a-half year old body, but not before finding its way into his brain, damaging his optical nerve, and permanently impairing his vision.

By age three, Easten had spent the majority of his life in a hospital, hooked up to machines, having to endure painful spinal taps and drugs so powerful he sometimes slept 23 hours a day. Through it all, though, he never once complained, was always excited to see visitors, and quick to laugh and smile. The nurses would fight for who got to care for Easten on their shifts because of his charming and positive way of brightening everyone's day.

Things haven't changed much over the last three years in this regard. The cancer has stayed at bay, and Easten remains a ray of light to everyone around him. Happy and healthy, he is able to navigate around his world despite having vision that requires him to hold a tablet to the tip of his nose to see anything.

I've never once heard Easten complain about taking medicine, getting shots, or having lost his vision and he always seems to find a reason to laugh and smile.

Sometimes, when I visit, he'll wander up near me, and ask, "Is that you Daddy?"

"No, Easten," I reply, "it's Uncle Andrew."

"Oh, hi, uncle Andrew; what are you eating?"

"I'm having some chips and salsa Easten. Would you like some?"

"Oh yes, thank you Uncle Andrew."

Easten loves his food and never misses an opportunity for a quick snack as he runs around the house trying to keep up with his big brother and older cousins.

Aside from all the running around. He also loves to ice skate and downhill ski—with a bit of help from his dad, draws and spends hours playing with his toys in his free time. Most importantly, he never ceases to give everyone around him a reason to smile.

His parents, grateful to have life in hospitals behind them and back to a normal functioning family, are thrilled the cancer is behind them and that Easten can enjoy himself and live his best life.

Easten is an inspiration to me and to everyone around him. Even though he would never understand why, he is the most popular little guy in his community. Everyone knows his name and everything about his story, since they were such a big part of his care and recovery. He is a sweet and kind soul who never hesitates to check in with everyone around him to make sure they are doing okay, and of course, to find out what they're eating.

Despite having lived through some of the most difficult circumstances, Easten personifies finding the positives in the negatives. His love and enthusiasm for life are contagious; his spirit touches everyone around him, and I always find myself smiling as I watch him go by.

Summary of Steps:

1. **Reaffirm Your Ideal Outcome** - What's The Goal? What does success look like for this goal?
2. **Identify The Negatives** - Write down the negative thoughts, doubts, and worries that are a concern due to the setback.
3. **Take Positive Actions** – list concrete actions you will take to achieve your goals.

Everyone experiences negative thoughts, reactions, and feelings, it is natural and unavoidable. High performers, however, don't dwell on them unnecessarily and quickly refocus onto the positives in the situation and the constructive actions they will take to still succeed—even when things seem bleak.

Let's Make This Stick

1. Make note of something fairly recent that hasn't gone your way—think of a situation where you failed, experienced a setback, or wanted a better outcome:

_____

_____

_____

2. Write down any negative thoughts, doubts, and worries that come to mind when you think about **Question 1.** In addition, list out any of the related emotions that you notice too.

_____

_____

_____

3. Reaffirm what you originally wanted in the situation. If things had gone in the ideal way, what would that have looked like and what would have happened? Describe it here:

_____

_____

_____

_____

4. Remember: positive actions are far more powerful than negative thoughts. List one positive action you will take for each negative thought you identified in **Question 3.** In addition, is there anything that you need to change in another area of your life to increase your chances of success? For example, stopping or reducing a negative habit of some kind? Or, decreasing your time with something else so you can devote it to these newly identified positive actions?

_____

_____

_____

_____

_____

CHAPTER 10

Say YES to Fear

And Keep Going!

Has fear ever made you falter, go in the wrong direction, or stood in the way of what you wanted to achieve? Few people could honestly answer no to a question like this. Fear is part of the wiring of a healthy human being; it's something we have to learn to live and work with if we want to be successful in our pursuits.

For the first twenty-eight years of my life, my fear seemed more like a mortal enemy to me than a useful emotion. Yes, it made a point of letting me know when I was in danger or at risk, but it also seemed to make some important things a lot harder than they needed to be.

My fear seemed to be constantly in the way when something was important to me. There were plenty of times when I was afraid to fail, make a mistake, or look bad, and decided it was best to just play it safe and not try. I remember once wanting a raise at work but being too scared to ask. I thought it might negatively impact my relationship with my boss and I worried the answer would be no, so I simply never bothered. Not trying was the easy way out. The only person who was worse off because I gave into my fear was me.

When I was in my first year of college, I was interested in someone who I had never met before. It was an awkward daily ritual. I'd see her in the halls and stare until she noticed me, then I'd panic and look away when she did. I wanted to meet her but was too afraid to take that first step and introduce myself.

Even though I thought about it and tried to find the courage for months, in the end I chickened out. I let my fear block me from doing what I really wanted because I worried the answer would be "no thanks," or worse.

The bottom line is I gave into my fear and missed out on the chance to find out if she would have been interested. It was a tough lesson. I learned that avoiding my fear meant missing out on opportunities.

There were also times when my fear showed up as intense nervousness prior to something important, like a job interview, presentation, or competition. In my early twenties, I had to give a presentation at a local car dealership. My place of work was hoping they would sponsor an event we were hosting, so they sent me in.

I had never done a sales pitch before and was really nervous. I saw my fear in this situation as a problem and kept wondering when it would go away so I could relax and do a good job of getting my points across. Of course, the opposite happened since I was fighting against my fear. I was so nervous I could barely think straight and found it to be a huge distraction. I rushed through my material and couldn't wait to get out of there. Unsurprisingly, they didn't end up sponsoring the event.

To summarize, for many years in certain areas of my life, my fear felt like an obstacle I'd be better off without. Unfortunately, I didn't clearly understand at the time how to *hear the fear* and do something constructive about it or to say YES to the fear and keep going, so it often got the better of me.

If we don't work constructively with our fear, it becomes much harder to get through. It can feel like an overwhelming and unnecessary barrier between us and our desired success. More importantly, letting fear take over can mean missing out on opportunities to get the most out of our lives.

Changing Our Approach to Fear

Fortunately, there was a distinct moment when my relationship with my fear started to change—it was during a game of Ultimate, to be exact, but more on that in a moment.

My main athletic pursuits growing up were soccer and ice hockey. I played both sports a ton, dabbling on the side with a bit of running, baseball, and squash. As a young adult, my time in these activities gave way to some lesser-known sports, one of which was "Ultimate." Apparently, whoever invented it figured it was the best game ever.

Admittedly, they may have been right for me. Ultimate had all the elements of a sport I liked: catching and throwing skills, strategy, and a healthy cardiovascular component. Think American

Football but with a disc instead of a ball, no tackling, and a lot more passing on every play.

I couldn't wait for game days. I'd usually show up early to practice throwing the "disc" (what Ultimate aficionados called their Frisbees) and to talk tactics endlessly with my teammates.

One characteristic of ultimate is that if you aren't one of the main throwers on the team, the game usually involves a lot of running after the disc. I was explaining this to a friend one day who had never heard of Ultimate before. He nodded his head in understanding and then asked, "Okay, I think I get it. So, were you the man or the dog?"

I hesitated for a second, seeing the corner he was trapping me in, before grudgingly replying, "Uh… I guess the dog?"

Not entirely sure how he tricked me into saying that, but in any event, it painted the right picture; I usually did a lot of sprinting most games to chase down and catch the disc.

I can vividly remember one particular game where I ended up covering an opponent on the other team who was clearly younger and in much better shape than I was. I had taken some extended time away from the game, so this was my first one in a while. I'm not sure if it was all the sitting around or one too many chocolate chip cookies during my time off, but I struggled to keep up with this jackrabbit of a human being as he ran around the field.

After what felt like an eternity, the point finally ended. I couldn't get to the sidelines fast enough. My lungs were burning like they were on fire, and I laid there on the ground, huffing and puffing. Any pretense of having handled the exertion well had long gone out the window as I lay there waiting for my strength to return. *That was both excruciating and not fun*, I thought to myself.

Naturally, it came with some good-natured ribbing from my teammates. Nothing wrong with a little public shaming every now and then to keep us humble.

Tool #1: Hear the Fear and Do Something About It!

Fortunately, the experience of not being able to keep up that day led to two key changes in my relationship with fear. The first was understanding that I could use the humbling experience in a positive way.

From that day forward, whenever I needed any motivation, all I had to do was think about how much I hated the feeling of being completely exhausted due to competing against a fitter opponent. Instantly, a wave of fear would shoot through my body and within a minute, my sneakers were laced up and off I'd go for a run. I was able to use my fear constructively to motivate myself to do the hard physical training needed to avoid a repeat of the situation.

If we want more success in our lives, then being able to use fear positively to achieve our goals is a critical skill. This illustrates our **first tool** in this chapter: **Hear the fear and do something about it.** By taking advantage of the fight-or-flight emotional reactions that fear evokes, we can use the resulting energy and increased motivation to take the necessary steps to achieve our goals.

I remember when my son Jack was around eleven years old and agonizing over the prospect of failing one of his upcoming school tests.

He kept walking around, moaning about how worried he was that he would fail. He acted like it was a foregone conclusion and that there wasn't anything he could do about it. My wife quickly set him straight. "Well, if you're so worried, do something about it. Get upstairs, and start studying." It snapped Jack out of his panic, and while it took a lot of reminders, we eventually got him into the mindset that when you hear a specific fear in your mind, and you are in a position to do something about it, get on it!

Similarly, I remember playing on the front lawn of our house near the street with Jack back when he was a toddler. He was pretty unbalanced in his walking at the time, and he was also unpredictable. He had no concept of what a street was or that he could easily get hit by a car, so running out into the road at some random moment was always in the cards.

My fear certainly kept me on my toes. I watched Jack like a hawk to make sure he didn't run into the road at some random moment as half feral toddlers often do. Being worried about his safety meant some anxious moments, but I used it constructively and paid extra attention when it mattered most.

Our relationship with fear can be tumultuous. It isn't always rational, and its message is often delivered not unlike that of an overly anxious "helicopter" parent:

Fear: "YOU MIGHT GET HIT BY THAT CAR!"

Me: "Oh yeah, I better back up from the road and look before crossing."

Fear: "YOU'RE GOING TO GET YOURSELF FIRED AT WORK!"

Me: "Shoot, I better work hard to make sure they're happy with my performance."

Fear: "YOU'RE GOING TO BOMB THAT EXAM!

Me: "I really don't want to fail, I better start studying more!"

Fear: "HEY! DON'T BOMB THAT EXAM…"

Me: "You literally just told me the same thing two seconds ago."

Fear: "DON'T FORGET TO TURN OFF THE BURNER ON THE STOVE!"

Me: "I checked three times, we're good!"

Fear: "DID YOU FORGET TO LOCK THE DOOR?"

Me: "Why would you wait until ten minutes after I leave to tell me that???"

Responding constructively with positive actions can go a long way toward helping us live more optimally.

Tool #2: Say YES to Fear – and Keep Going!

While we may consciously register specific fears like the above, there are other times and situations where there isn't something we can specifically *do* about our fears in the moment. Sometimes we just have to continue forward, because not facing our fear isn't a viable option. Sure, we can avoid an important conversation we know we need to have, decline a job interview, or not show up for an exam, presentation, or a competition, but the consequences may bring more harm than good. Sometimes, it's the big moment, and we just have to keep going when fear hits.

This brings us to our **second tool: say YES to fear and keep going!** Let's take a closer look at how this simple yet powerful mental tool can help.

Step 1: Acknowledge Your Fear

The first step is used whenever you find yourself in a situation that makes you feel exceptionally nervous, fearful, or anxious. Any time an emotion like this comes up intensely enough to distract you from what you're doing, start by acknowledging it. You can do this by responding mentally with, "Yes, I feel nervous," or "Yes, I feel scared," or "Yes, I feel anxious," etc. This encourages us to accept our emotional responses instead of fighting them. It helps these emotions feel more manageable and gives us the confidence to get through them and reach our goals.

Step 2: Keep Going!

The second step to saying YES to fear is to refocus and continue moving forward with what you're trying to do.

I remember being really nervous about introducing a well-known author to an audience of over 400 people at an event I created and hosted about fifteen years ago. It was my first time speaking in front of so many people and I was afraid to make a mistake and embarrass myself.

The closer it got, the more nervous I became. In the end, knowing I had no choice, I got up and started speaking. It went okay, but it wasn't necessarily my best presentation. I vividly remember struggling as my focus shot back and forth between thinking about my fear and concentrating on what I was trying to say. Had I said yes, I am nervous, committed to moving forward no matter if I stumbled or made a mistake, and focused on what I was doing, I would have had a much better experience and performance.

Using "Hear the Fear and Do Something About it," and "Say YES to Fear and Keep Going," in Real-Life Situations

I was once asked to do a presentation for the Board of Directors at my place of work in the early years of my management career. I was instantly nervous about it. Not only would my boss be watching, but so would my fellow senior managers—not to mention the board members themselves.

Just thinking about it weeks beforehand made me anxious. I was again afraid to make a mistake, embarrass myself, and negatively impact my career.

My **first step** was to make use of all the energy my body was producing from my nerves to prepare thoroughly for the presentation and know my material inside and out. All the nervous energy gave me plenty of motivation to research and ensure I had all the stats top of mind. I did something about it.

I also planned what to do if I felt extra nervous when it started, which was to get up and physically move around in the space during my presentation.

I got even more nervous the day of the presentation, especially when I got there and waited for my turn to speak, but it was manageable. I kept acknowledging it with a "Yes, I'm nervous," "Yes, I'm afraid to fail," "Yes, I'm scared," and so on as needed. I just hoped how I felt wasn't as obvious to everyone else as it was to me!

When I finally walked into the room, the atmosphere was a lot more casual than I had expected, which helped me relax. I must have been imagining a scene of a judge and jury in my mind, but by the time I started speaking, I focused on what I had to say, and everything flowed. Any nerves were gone in a minute or two. People in the audience appeared engaged and asked a bunch of good questions at the end. I was relieved, happy it went well, and grateful that I used my fear constructively.

Saying YES Helps us Work with Our Emotions Instead of Against Them

So why does saying YES to our fear work? For starters, we stop seeing our fear as a problem and trying to avoid it, which only compounds the situation. By acknowledging our fear, we stop wasting energy struggling against it. Instead, we learn to use that energy positively, like doing something about it and preparing ahead of time. By acknowledging our fear, we can get on with focusing on the task at hand.

A good friend named Riley once told me that job interviews always made him feel sickly nervous. I suggested he try using the "say YES to fear" tool before the interview. He tried it out whenever the fear came up to help himself get through his nerves. "Yes, I feel nervous," "Yes, I'm scared I won't interview well," "Yes, I'm afraid they won't like me," and so on. He kept going each time fear came up. By saying yes to his fear, the interview became more manageable.

Riley felt more confident and focused before and during interviews from then on. He was able to concentrate on the things he needed to do to succeed instead of fixating on his fear. He tells me he still uses this tool to this day, any time he finds herself in similar situations that make him nervous.

Hearing the Fear and Deciding Not To Act—For Now

None of the above tools or examples suggest we *always* have to go through our fear. There may well be times when we consciously decide we're not ready to do something yet and that's perfectly okay.

As mentioned earlier, fear warns us of things that threaten us in some way listening at these times might be in our best interest. Our fear also lets us know our emotional limits and can flag experiences we're not ready for just yet.

There might be times when we don't feel ready or capable enough yet for a particular undertaking. We might have skills or emotional capacities that we still need to improve for us to succeed, and our fear can help us sense that. There is nothing wrong with deciding to wait for a time when we feel more ready—if we have the option.

One of my favorite examples of this is from Alex Honnold, an American rock climber who is famous for his free solo ascents (climbing without equipment and ropes). He is known for being the first person to free solo climb El Capitan, a three-thousand-foot mountain face in Yosemite National Park.

Alex spent over a year preparing for the climb. In 2016, he aborted his first attempt to complete it because he just didn't feel ready yet. Finally, on June 3, 2017, without notifying anyone on his team, his confidence was there and he decided to go for it. He summited and finally realized his dream to free solo climb El Capitan. Alex had to know when he was ready to take on this enormous risk and only he could intuit when that was.

There may be times we're not yet ready to go through our fears. When we have the option to wait, we can continue to practice and prepare like Alex did until it feels like the right time to try.

Fear Isn't Supposed to Go Away- We Need It!

To be clear, the intention of saying YES to our fear isn't supposed to make it go away. It's meant to make sure we use the resulting energy constructively. Saying YES helps us refocus on the positive outcome we hope for. Trying to make our fear go away is like signing up for an internal wrestling match we're guaranteed to lose. Saying YES to fear is about accepting our emotions and using the energy that fear evokes to empower our performance to a higher level with increased focus and concentration. As you make a habit of this and it becomes a part of your process, fear becomes more manageable.

Fear will always be there; it's an integral part of us and we need it to survive. When used constructively, it keeps us focused on what's important to us and propels us to a higher level of focus and engagement.

If we are prepared to acknowledge our fear and take positive action, we are on our way to harnessing the resulting energy to perform at our best.

Fear is vital for our survival. We need it. Without a healthy dose of fear, we might find ourselves getting a little too close to the edge of a cliff or forgetting to look both ways before crossing a street. We not only need our fear to keep us alive, we also need it to motivate us to put in the work to avoid failing. When we learn to use our fear constructively, we are well on our way to supercharging our climb toward a High-Performing Mind.

Two Tools To Use Your Fear to Power Through to Success:

Tool #1: Hear the Fear and Do Something About it!

Tool #2: Say YES to your fear and Keep Going!

This brings us to the end of Chapter 10, you've nearly completed your climb and are well on your way to having a high-performing mind. We're nearly there!

You have clarity about what you want, you're armed with some discipline, understand things won't always be easy and have the resilience to get past any setbacks and failures along the way.

You are building stronger emotional armor, you're focused on the process, and are able to find the positives in your negatives when you feel stuck or aren't making progress. You now also understand your fear a little better and can use it to power you through to your goals.

Let's find out how to consistently perform at our best so you can get better results and be successful more often by using present moment focus to access flow next in Chapter 11.

Let's Make This Stick

Summary of Steps To Use Your Fear To Help You Succeed:

Step 1- Say YES to your fear and repeat it any time needed: "Yes I'm scared," "yes, I'm afraid to fail," "yes, I feel anxious, worried," etc.

Step 2- Use the energy your body is producing from feeling scared as motivation to take positive actions to improve your chances to succeed.

Step 3- Say YES, and go through the fear, refocus on what you want, and in the immortal words of Nike: "Just Do It!"

1. List three things that you're scared might happen, or three situations that you are afraid of. Start each list with the word YES. For example, "Yes, I'm scared I might fail," or "Yes, I'm afraid of looking bad while public speaking," etc.:

i. _____

ii. _____

iii. _____

2. List three positive actions you can take that will contribute to your success with each of these situations you listed above. What are you going to do about it?

i. _____

ii. _____

iii. _____

3. Say YES, keep going, refocus on what you want, and in the immortal words of Nike: "Just Do It!" Identify an upcoming situation where you can plan to say YES to fear and keep going:

_____

_____

_____

CHAPTER 11

Performing at Our Best

Using Present Moment Focus
To Access "Flow"

In my college days, I lived about twenty minutes up the highway from campus, so I drove myself to and from school. One winter afternoon when I was getting ready to leave after a long day of classes, three of my friends from the neighborhood asked me for a lift back home. A big snowstorm had just started, which usually meant a slow commute back to town.

The four of us crammed into my undersized Volkswagen hatchback. The snow and ice were already covering the road, so I drove slowly as we crossed campus and headed for the highway. The cold temperatures combined with nonstop talking from four exuberant teenagers made concentrating a challenge. The fog kept building up on the windows even with the heat and defrost on full blast.

When we finally got to the highway, traffic was at a standstill and backed up for miles. We sat there for ages, hardly moving. Seeing we weren't getting anywhere, I got the bright idea to follow a few cars that had started cutting over a low median to a nearby side road. Bypassing the huge backlog of traffic seemed like a great idea to my eighteen-year-old brain. "We could save an hour of sitting around," I reasoned. Was it questionable? Definitely. Illegal? Undoubtedly. But it was the '90s after all, so I decided to ignore any protests from my common sense and go for it.

With the music blaring, nonstop chatter, and joking around, I pulled over to the right side of the highway. I then slowly edged the car up onto an ankle-high median that divided the highway from the side road.

The median was about as wide as my Volkswagen was long. Cars and trucks whizzed past the nose of my car at near highway speeds as I waited for an opening to get to the side road. I vividly remember craning my head around my friend in the front passenger seat to look out his fogged window through the thick falling snow for any oncoming traffic.

Just as I thought things had cleared up enough to make a dash to the side road and lifted my foot toward the accelerator, I jammed full force on the brakes instead—a fraction of a second before coming off the median. We all lurched forward in our seat belts as the car came to an abrupt stop and an eighteen-wheel transport truck went flying past, just inches from the front bumper.

To this day, I'm still not sure what caught my eye or made me hit the brakes, but with my heart pounding with the realization of how close we just came to instant death, it was a major wake-up call.

Unsurprisingly, "take two" to get off the median and reach the side road went a lot differently. The fun and games were now over. With the radio off and in complete silence, we all stared intently at the road through rolled-down windows to make sure we could *actually* see. Nobody cared about the sub-zero temperature or the snow falling into the car. I didn't go until we all agreed—at least five times each—that the coast was clear, and no trucks were speeding our way.

With the adrenaline still pumping through my veins, and my level of alertness ratcheted up the equivalent of ten espressos, I drove the remainder of the way home. I could count the number of times I blinked on one hand, and I was hyper-aware of every inch of road and flake of snow that went by my windshield. I drove as carefully as I could and didn't relax my concentration until my last passenger was safely home and I pulled into my driveway.

Accessing "Flow"

It's interesting how a combination of fear and adrenaline can result in incredible focus when something threatens our survival. After nearly getting my friends and I taken out by a transport truck, we were certainly far more dialed into avoiding any repeats of the incident. I became 100% focused on getting home safely and my mind was free from any distractions. Whether I was aware of it at the time or not, I had accessed an elevated state of mind known as "flow", which gave me the ability to exceed my normal levels of focus, concentration, and performance.

Fortunately, it isn't necessary to nearly get hit by a transport truck or experience some type of life-threatening crisis to tap into this elevated human potential. Any time something matters to us, there's a possibility to access flow—a mental state of neurological clarity, coordination, and heightened concentration, which allows us to perform at our peak capabilities.

Flow can be described in many ways. People often refer to having clarity about what needs to be done to succeed and how to do it. Time seems to slow down, and objects can appear bigger, more vibrant, and more detailed than usual. Being *in* a state of flow allows us to use all our mental, emotional, and physical resources to perform at a higher level, which is often referred to as a "peak performance." We can become so immersed in what we're doing while in a state of deep flow that we aren't conscious of thinking; it can feel like nothing else exists in the moment.

Aron Ralston, the famous American climber, summarized being in flow well, "You are not thinking ahead. You are just thinking about what is in front of you each second."

I can personally recall a handful of times, while competing in sports back in the day and on the brink of defeat, when I was able to find extra energy, focus, and insight into what I needed to do to succeed that I didn't have previously. In these flow moments, I was able to move with a quickness, coordination, and purpose that allowed me to perform significantly better than my usual.

Fortunately, accessing flow isn't reserved for athletes or sports. In a similar way, I can also recall intense conversations, exams, presentations, meetings, and interviews where I found a clarity in my thinking and communication abilities that were beyond what I would see from myself on a regular basis. In these situations, flow seemed to just happen, and I wasn't sure why or how to get back to it.

Finding flow and performing at our best can be an elusive experience that seems hard to replicate. Something we remember wistfully, recalling how remarkably things went and how focused we were in those moments. But how did we get into flow states in the first place and is there a way to harness this in our daily lives? Is this something just reserved for critical moments? How else can we benefit from flow? Is there a way we can take advantage of these heightened states of mind and perform at our best on a more regular basis?

Yes, is the short answer to this last question, and we will explore each of these questions further, but before we do, let's take a step back and ask ourselves why we would want to access flow and perform at our best in the first place.

Why Does Performing at Our Best Matter?

Performing at our best greatly enhances our chances of getting better results and outcomes in the things that we do and care about. No doubt, we are all familiar with times when things didn't go as well as we hoped, and we left a situation scratching our heads and wondering what and how we could have done better.

Performing at our best can mean better outcomes, more daily successes in more areas of our lives, and help us enjoy our lives more because more things go well. Performing well can be the difference between success and failure.

When we perform at our best, conversations go better in our personal lives and at work. This leads to smoother experiences and better results. It means our presentations get better, we do better on exams and in interviews, we perform at our best in our athletics and pursuits, we're more productive and creative at work, in our hobbies, and engaged in our relationships with others. In short, it means we deliver and succeed in those success defining moments of our lives. We experience more positive experiences, more often, and live happier and more fulfilling lives.

Whenever we bring our full concentration to our activities, we instantly begin to perform better. When we have this focus, we generally see better results than when we only give half an effort, attempt to multitask, or get sidetracked by distractions. I can think of a few occasions where I got distracted when someone was talking to me and then had no idea what they were asking when they were suddenly waiting for the answer. "Oops, sorry I'm not quite clear about what you're asking," I've admitted. Only then fully aware I hadn't really been listening.

Being fully engaged and present can make us feel more alive and feel transformational. If we took the time to really listen when others spoke, our understanding would increase, we would remember instructions better, and they would feel heard and appreciated. What would that attentiveness do for the relationships in our lives? People aren't generally impressed when someone is there in body, but their minds seem to be a million miles away, or when they appear less interested in the conversation than with their phones.

Being fully engaged in the present moment has been critical for me to have successfully navigated some of the most challenging moments of my life. Without having found varying degrees of my best performance at these times, I would never have made my way through many life-defining situations as successfully.

The benefits of finding flow and performing at our best becomes more obvious when we think about our pursuits. If we really brought our full mental, emotional, and physical resources to each activity, our performance would increase immensely, our error rates would decrease, and we would gain greater insight into what we needed to do to succeed.

In those key moments when we want the best possible results so we can achieve our goals—in competition, in an interview, during an exam, or a presentation, or before an important meeting or conversation—using all of our physical, mental, and emotional resources to perform at our best will certainly go a long way in maximizing our chances for success.

In addition, when we are perceived as being high performing by others, it leads to more opportunities. We aren't likely to get tapped for that promotion, high-paying job, or make that top team if we aren't perceived as being high-performing in some way.

Mental and Emotional Strength and Stability

We all have a tendency to get distracted by the things that go wrong, stuck in our minds, ruminate about our concerns, and wind ourselves up emotionally in ways that aren't always productive, let alone, high performing. These states of mind generally don't lead to feeling good or to the best outcomes.

The quickest remedy for this—and to find increased calmness and levelheadedness—is found in using what I refer to as "present moment focus." This is the simple process of fully focusing on what we are doing and being mentally in the present moment.

Being fully engaged in what we are doing also increases our mental and emotional stability. Keeping our minds firmly focused on the task at hand reduces our brain's tendency to dwell on things from our past or worry about what could happen in the future. By having a present moment focus, it helps us to feel calmer and let go of emotionally charged thoughts and emotions. Doing this allows the mind to stop focusing on negative thoughts and feelings, and instead concentrate on what's going on around us.

Any time I find myself getting caught up in emotional responses or excessive worry, really attending to what I'm doing is a quick way to dissipate these distractions and let things go. Just a few minutes of repeatedly bringing your mind back to what you're doing is enough to notice the results. It can be thought of as a form of meditation in action.

I remember when my son Jack was about six-years-old and struggling with nightmares and being frightened at night. He told me he kept waking up and thinking about scary things he had seen in movies and how he couldn't stop it. I pointed out these thoughts came from the past and suggested he focus on his stuffed animals instead. "Whenever you start thinking of those scary things, instead, think about how your stuffed animals look and feel right now."

I didn't expect it to work so quickly, but he didn't mention it again. A couple of weeks later, I asked if he was still having the same trouble at night, and he said, "No, thinking about my stuffies made it go away."

As the story illustrates, being present in the moment and focusing on what we are doing can improve many areas of our lives, no matter our age. And the good news is that we can learn to access this whenever we want. It might take a bit of extra effort, but the rewards of bringing our full attention to what we're doing is well-worth it to achieve the many benefits.

Using present moment focus to access mental states of flow is the quickest way to instantly improve our performance, feel calmer, get better results and hence, greater success and enjoyment in our lives.

Tool #1: Present Moment Focus

To enjoy these improvements in our lives, we need to bring that **present moment focus,** referenced above, to our tasks and activities. This means bringing 100% of our mental resources to what we are doing, seeing, and hearing and being sharply aware of what is happening in the present moment.

The more something matters to us and the more we want a particular result, the easier it is to achieve present moment focus, which is the gateway to states of flow and being at our best. This is because our emotions help us to engage more intensely. The longer we stay present to what is happening in the moment, the more deeply we find flow states of mind.

When we fear failing, for example, redirecting our focus to the outcome we want in the situation—instead of what we're afraid might happen—increases our engagement, and chances to achieve the outcome we want. When we bring 100% of our mental resources to what we are doing, we are able to access our best performances. These peak moments don't need to be reserved for life threatening situations, we can find them by using present moment focus in our daily lives as well.

I had to speak to a manager once who wasn't performing well at her job. It was a delicate situation. I knew from past experience that she was extremely sensitive to any feedback that wasn't positive. I started casually discussing one of my concerns with her performance, but within a few minutes, I realized things weren't going well and she was getting upset. A wave of fear hit me as I realized the conversation could end up being a complete disaster and make matters worse instead of better. Since there was no turning back at that point, I realized I had to bring an intense present moment focus to what I was saying, and how I was saying it.

Fortunately, my strong desire for things to go well, combined with bringing my full focus and concentration into the conversation, helped me communicate in the best way I could, and we ended on a positive note. My present moment focus helped me to find flow and elevate my level of attentiveness and communication. I became extremely focused on every detail of how she was receiving the information I was conveying. This helped me notice subtle emotional reactions in her facial expressions and body language. Being very engaged in the moment helped me navigate my way to a successful outcome.

I was playing tennis with a friend once and had one of those days where I missed my shots more than usual. I got increasingly frustrated as the match went on and started focusing on all my errors.

After a while, I was able to catch myself and use my desire to play better to engage in the game with more present moment focus. This helped me concentrate on what I needed to do to win instead of being distracted by everything I thought was going wrong. This resulted in finding more flow in my execution, higher overall performance, and consequently, better results.

Our ability to be in the present moment without dwelling on distracting thoughts and emotions for a *sustained period of time* brings us into neurological flow and therefore, higher levels of performance —no matter what we are doing.

When we have intense emotions related to what we are doing, like the feeling of really wanting to succeed, and combine that with a singular focus on the task at hand, this resulting present moment focus can reduce distracting thoughts and make it easier to maintain our concentration. The longer we can sustain an intense present moment focus, the more likely we are to find ourselves being at our best, which helps us navigate through challenging situations with far greater success.

There are many degrees of flow. There are those rare times where we go so deeply into flow that it can feel almost transcendental. During these times, our decision making and results are so good it can be surprising how well something goes. Other times, we touch into flow and up our performance during a significant moment like an event, exam, job interview, presentation, important conversation, or during competition—like I did with my tennis game that day.

We can't always control how deeply we go into flow, but any time we bring a present moment focus to what we're doing, we are destined for better life outcomes.

Tool #2: Champion Refocus —Mentally Preparing to Perform at Our Best

There are times in our lives, like in the situations we covered above, when being at our best is extremely important to us. In addition to harnessing our emotions and desire to succeed, flow can also be achieved from the right balance of physical relaxation, calmness, mental activation, and present moment focus. Combining these elements may seem complex, but it's easier than it sounds, and we will dive into how to do this later. First, let's talk about how to mentally prepare to be at our best when it matters most to us and we have those success defining moments.

Over the years, as a high-performing coach, I have often helped my athletes mentally prepare for a big game or tournament. All their training and routine mental preparation time and effort ahead of the big event aside, this is what it would look like to mentally prepare in the hour or two prior to their big moment.

It would begin with helping to ensure they had the needed clarity about their specific desires and goals for their upcoming competitive moment—just as we did in Chapters 1 and 6, when we identified your primary desire. In these athletes' cases, their primary objective was usually to win, though not always— if the competition was well above their level. In these situations, they might choose a different goal like giving a full effort until the end or scoring a certain number of points, etc.

Once this was established, we then moved into identifying the best mindsets the athlete would need—these were specific to each individual—but included being prepared for a challenge, staying positive, and ready to give 100% effort levels throughout the entire duration of the competition. These were achieved by referencing all their training and practice time, by recalling all their successful moments from the past, and by ensuring they had the required resilience.

Their resilience was amplified by going through some of the tools we identified in Chapter 2. Ensuring they expected that there would be hard moments, potential setbacks, and all kinds of possible distractions along the way. We also planned how they would refocus after each setback or distraction. Champions refocus extremely quickly, ensuring that they keep a positive mindset, and bring 100% of their full mental and emotional resources to every moment.

From there, once they were armed with resilience and prepared to use **our second tool, Champion Refocus**, they would also use a mental exercise, or two, to elevate their ability to have a present moment focus to start and throughout game time. These exercises will be detailed later in this chapter.

Once all these steps were completed, they ensured they were emotionally calm, physically relaxed, yet mentally alert and focused in the moment on the task at hand.

You may have noted as you've read this that the above is a very thorough preparation process and may not be realistic for everyone. It certainly isn't necessary to go through all of these steps to improve how well we do. Any one of the methods outlined above is sufficient to improve our performance and results.

As mentioned earlier, and throughout *A High-Performing Mind,* the above steps, the present-moment focus, and the mental preparation before "game time," are applicable to any situation we deem important enough to us that we want to be at our best and maximize our chances for success.

I have certainly gone through many of these steps prior to presentations, interviews, and important meetings. They all help, along with a present moment focus and champion refocus, for important moments to go as well and as smoothly as possible. This would also be the case for meetings, exams, and significant conversations.

How much mental preparation you choose to do and how many of these tools you decide to use is completely up to you. It will depend heavily on the circumstances, but most are standard practice for many of the world's top athletes and can benefit anyone at any time.

All Roads to Flow Pass Through Present Moment Focus

Present moment focus is the underlying factor that all moments of flow, and hence our ability to be at our best, have in common. Whatever methods we use to get there, being fully engaged in what we are doing, with a quiet mind that doesn't dwell on distractions, is what helps us to access flow and find our best performances.

As noted, things that elicit a strong emotional response—like a danger to our physical well-being or when something that really matters to us is on the line—can catapult us into flow very quickly.

Other times, when the situation doesn't generate as much urgency, it might take some extra effort and repeated refocus back to the task at hand to maintain a high degree of concentration. Like anything, we get better with practice. In time, we can find flow when we are relaxed and calm, but also mentally alert at the same time. A present moment focus is what helps to make these happen.

Despite there being a range of flow states and never knowing ahead of time how deeply we'll go on a given occasion, if we consider our normal baseline level of distraction and lack of focus, bringing our full 100% focus to the moment and achieving any degree of flow can instantly improve our life experiences.

Ultimately, accessing flow comes down to one thing: Being completely present and focused on what we're doing in the moment. When we become completely immersed, we become so consumed in our activity that there's no room to think or consider anything else—as Aron Rolsten so succinctly described.

It Won't Always Be Possible or Easy to Find Flow

Present moment focus, of course, is easier said than done or else it would be a common experience for everyone. There are so many distractions that can interrupt us from this laser-like attention: other tasks popping into our minds, our devices pinging us with a new notification, someone interrupting us, environment conditions during our activity, the thought of something immediately gratifying, having an off day, not feeling well, finding it harder than usual to concentrate, being tired, upset, scared, frustrated, nervous, needing to pee, seeing a fly on the wall, and on and on.

There's no shortage of ways we can lose our present moment focus, and the above examples don't even consider our self-sabotaging brain, which can inject any variety of distracting thoughts, worries, or ideas when we least want them.

Overthinking is another quick way to exit any semblance of flow. There's an old expression in sport: "Paralysis by analysis." This illustrates one of the quickest ways to ruin any flow we might have. An old coach of mine once put it well by saying, "When you play the piano, you need to listen to the sound of the music and not think about the individual keys to press." In other words, focusing on our objectives and not on the technical details while performing greatly enhances our results by helping us find flow. If we're trying to perform a skill well, then the more we can do that skill without thinking about it the better.

There will also, inevitably, be times when no matter what we do, we just can't find any flow on a particular day. If this happens, no need to belabor the effort to find it, we just let it go and do our best with what we have in that particular moment in time.

Four Mental Exercises to Get Into Flow

Given the infinite ways we can lose our present moment focus and exit states of flow, using some exercises and strategies before and during our important moments, as illustrated above, can greatly increase our ability to bring our full present moment focus to what we are doing. These exercises can also help us get back into a present moment flow quickly when we lose it.

Our four mental exercises are:

1- Practicing Systematic Body Relaxation
2- Using Sensory Perception Feedback
3- Using Keywords and Consciously Breathing
4- Refocusing After Distractions.

Let's take a more detailed look at what these are and how each would be used.

Mental Exercise #1: Practicing Systematic Body Relaxation

Systematic body relaxation is used primarily <u>before</u> an important moment to let go of physical tension, quiet the mind, and reduce overthinking. When we carry unnecessary tension in our muscles, we impede the smoothness of our actions. Tension over activates muscle groups that may not be needed to the same extent as others, hence reducing our coordination and fluidity of movement. Muscular tension can also increase emotional tension, so relaxing our muscles can be a great way to help us feel calmer.

I've personally used systematic body relaxation for many years and shared the technique with clients who have found it highly beneficial. It can be used before any activity, from athletic pursuits to presentations, exams, job interviews, and more.

One of my favorite methods to achieve systematic body relaxation is using something called progressive muscle relaxation, which was invented by Dr. Edmund Jacobson in the 1920s. There are several online video guides that walk through this method, and it can be done in a number of ways. Let's go through one together.

Give it a try now: Get up and walk very slowly and consciously somewhere that you have some extra space. While walking, start by thinking about how your head and particularly your face feels. As you do this, take a deep, conscious breath slowly in and out, and let go of any tension you can sense in these areas by physically trying to relax them.

Continue this process by relaxing your eyes. Again, breathing in and out slowly and letting go of any tension you can sense around them. Continue to the mouth and tongue, with the same deep breath in and out, and again let go of any tension.

Then progress downwards, with the muscles in the throat, the back of your neck, your shoulders, back, chest, stomach, and glutes. Relax each of these using conscious breathing and releasing tension. Continue to the legs, focusing on the muscles in both the front and back, finally ending with your feet and toes. How do you feel when you're done?

By the time this exercise is complete, we generally feel calmer and more relaxed. Our minds have slowed down and we are one step closer to being in a state of flow, because throughout this practice we have been paying attention to how each body part feels. This attention to each body part channels our minds toward a present moment focus to provide this feedback, consequently helping us achieve flow states.

Systematic physical relaxation is also a great stress reliever and can be done in a sitting position as well. I generally recommend doing it for five to fifteen minutes for optimal effect. I avoid doing this exercise lying down, because it's also a quick way to fall asleep!

Now if you're about to engage in an important activity after completing your systematic muscle relaxation, be sure to remind yourself how much you want to succeed. The goal of this first exercise is to find calmness and relaxation, but to perform at a high-level, you'll also need to ensure your mental intensity remains focused on your goal.

By coupling this strong desire and a highly activated mind with relaxation and emotional calmness, you will greatly enhance your present moment focus and ability to perform at your best at anything including in sports, at work, during presentations, interviews, exams, meetings, while interacting with others and so on.

Mental Exercise #2: Sensory Perception Feedback

Using our senses is another powerful way to increase our engagement in the present moment. You can utilize this tool to promote calmness and reduce mental chatter prior to something you want to perform well at. You can also use it to refocus if there are any breaks in the action during an important event. If you find yourself with a few seconds or minutes of downtime before continuing your performance, you can use this exercise to bring your mind back into flow.

Sensory perception feedback starts by consciously asking ourselves what we are currently perceiving in our environments by using our vision, hearing, and sense of touch— one at a time.

Give it a try it now: Start by asking yourself what you can *visually see* around you in this moment. You might notice multiple objects but choose one and specifically focus on details you might normally overlook.

For example, right now you can probably look at a wall and notice the color, the texture, the size, and any cracks and imperfections. You would then repeat this process with a second object like a table, or the ceiling, or by looking out the window at a tree, the grass, etc. Anything will do.

Simply look and make mental notes of as much visual information about the object as you can. The more unusual the detail you notice the better. By doing this, you're requiring your mind to use present moment focus to provide the information you're looking for.

Continue this process by next thinking about what you can *hear*.

Give it a try now: Sit quietly and make note of anything you can hear. Maybe you notice the buzz of an appliance or light fixture, people's voices, air going through a vent, the wind, a bird chirping, a car engine, or the silence. Again, it doesn't matter what you hear, but as you listen, your mind comes to a present moment focus to ascertain the information.

The third time you repeat this exercise you'll be using your sense of touch.

Give it a try now: Touch a nearby object and mentally make note of what you feel. Is it smooth or rough? Is it cold or warm to the touch? Is it hard or soft or somewhere in between? How dry or damp does it feel?

You can repeat this process using any one of your senses at a time and repeat it for as long as is necessary for your mind to quiet and find that present moment focus.

Just a few minutes of consciously using our senses to acquire extra specific details about our environments can make us feel more relaxed and calmer and give us a present moment focus that brings us quickly into a state of flow. We can then maintain this flow through any upcoming activities.

Mental Exercise #3: Using Keywords and Consciously Breathing

As we gain experience with what it feels like to be in the present moment, using keywords and consciously breathing can be a quick and effective way to focus, calm ourselves, and come back to the present. Keywords have long been a tool used by professional and Olympic athletes to increase concentration during competition and as a gateway to finding their best performances. But anyone at any time can use keywords to draw their attention back to the present moment.

You can use keywords with conscious breathing prior to an important event or during periods of downtime while performing. A keyword is any word you can use that brings your focus back to the task at hand. You would say your keyword, followed by slowly breathing in and out.

For example, I have often used the word "here" to draw my attention to the immediate environment around me. This helps prevent my mind from wandering and reminds me to stay present wherever I am. I then take a slow, deep breath while looking around and soaking in everything that I observe nearby. I repeat this same sequence: Mentally saying my keyword "here" and taking a slow, conscious breath while looking around. I repeat this exercise as many times as needed to feel my mind slow down and become more focused on my immediate environment and the present moment.

After a few repetitions, I usually change my keyword to "now." I find this word also helps me draw my attention to what I'm doing at the time and prevents my mind from wandering into the past or future and getting distracted. Again, I follow my keyword with a slow, deep breath, then repeat the whole sequence as often as desired.

Give it a try now: Mentally say the word "here" and take a slow, conscious breath while looking around the room. Repeat this five times, consciously breathing each time.

Now try the exercise again, this time using the word "now" with a slow conscious breath in and out. Repeat this sequence five times. After several repetitions, you'll start to feel calmer, more relaxed, and more present.

These two keywords are suggestions for where to start. Feel free to make your keyword anything that works for you. Choose any word that draws your attention back to the present. It's helpful to use one word at a time and follow it with a slow breath in and out before repeating it again or choosing another word.

Other keywords could be helpful reminders while performing, such as "relax," "calm," "be present," "this moment," "take your time," "breathe," "look around," "be ready," etc. This technique can work for anyone at any time to refocus and quiet the mind into the present moment. What keyword you use comes down to personal preference and finding what works, so experiment away!

Just a few minutes of using a keyword and consciously breathing can greatly enhance our ability to find flow and sustain it.

Mental Exercise #4: Champion's Refocus - Refocusing After Distractions

Redirecting our minds back to the present moment is a critical tool for success and for sustaining flow and our ability to perform near our best. Most of us will experience distractions that divert our attention away from what we're doing 95% of the time. Whatever the distraction, it's in our best interest to become reabsorbed in our activity as quickly as possible. Refocusing helps us sustain our flow and avoid any extended downturns as we aim to deliver our best.

How do we refocus? As soon as you notice you've lost focus, immediately redirect your attention back to what you were doing. Use the realization that you've lost focus as a prompt to bring your mind back to the present. If you're working on a project, and you notice you're daydreaming or you get the urge to check your messages, use the distraction as a reminder to bring your attention back to the activity at hand. "Oh yes, I'm supposed to be focusing right now!"

Refocusing doesn't mean not taking breaks when you need them. But if you know it's time to focus and accomplish a task, then redirecting back after a distraction can help you to find the present moment focus and flow we're looking for.

Any one of the first three mental exercises—systematic muscle relaxation, using keywords while consciously breathing, and sensory perception feedback—can also be used to redirect yourself back into a state of flow when you lose it. Having to recover lost focus, even dozens of times during an activity, is completely normal.

Embracing Not Thinking

Once we're in a state of flow, we no longer need to consciously think of releasing muscular tension, determining what information our senses are bringing to us, and using keywords while breathing. Our minds have been primed by these tools, so we shift our focus to what we are doing and bring our full concentration to it. Remember, bringing our present moment focus intensely to what we are doing is key to improving outcomes.

To avoid coming out of flow prematurely, not thinking about it can keep us in a flow state. That includes not remarking about how well things are going to ourselves or others halfway through a task. That's a sure way to find ourselves sinking back down to earth… no longer in a flow state.

When I played doubles squash with some fellow pros for fun, every once in a while someone would go on a hot streak for a game or two and hit a bunch of winning shots. As soon as one of the guys noticed someone in "the zone," they'd start saying things to make the person think about it. "Wow, John, you're really playing well. You've hit that backhand winner a number of times today. How are you doing that?" Sure enough, that's all it took for John to start thinking about it and for his hot streak to come to an abrupt end.

Wasn't this a bit mean? Yes, but all in good fun. It was also effective—even when we knew what the person was up to. More importantly, this simple example illustrates the point: it's best not to think about flow when we find ourselves in it.

This can be the case for areas outside of sports when we are aiming to perform well. During interviews, presentations, important meetings, and conversations, I avoid assessing how I'm doing or have done until it's over.

A Little Practice Goes a Long Way

Practicing the four mental exercises of this chapter during regular, noncritical activities can help us develop our present moment focus so that it's easily accessible when we do need it. Conversations with people are a great place to start practicing, since speaking is such a common part of life. Next time you're chatting with someone, listen carefully when they're talking and really pay attention to everything they say. Try using your keywords to refocus on the here and now whenever you become distracted or notice your mind wandering.

Transitions in our day-to-day lives provide another opportunity to practice these tools. Any brief period of downtime, like waiting for a bus, heading out to the car, walking into another room, or going up or down the stairs are good moments to practice any of the four mental exercises. Little opportunities like these give us a chance to develop a present moment focus so it's strong and accessible when we need to perform at our best.

It takes extra effort to bring a present moment focus to the things we do, and it can be a challenge at times. But once we have a little practice under our belts, the benefits start to become apparent. Before we know it, we're calmer, more focused, and less distracted. At some point, we might end up being so absorbed in what we're doing that we look up to find that time has flown by, and we've been incredibly productive.

How we feel about our performance is the best measure of success. Better results, greater productivity, fewer lapses in our concentration, and using champion refocus to get back on track more quickly are all signs we're on the right track.

It's important to remember that there may be times when taking a break and forgetting about being present is exactly what we need. There's nothing wrong with coming back to it another day when we find it to be a strain or we need to recharge.

Accept what's going wrong and stay focused on what you want. Distractions and setbacks will always be part of life, but our ability to refocus and stay present longer will gradually improve, strengthening like a muscle. As we start to experience improved outcomes from a higher functioning mind, it won't take much to inspire us to use present moment focus as a regular feature in our lives. Going through our days focused on each thing we do not only dramatically improves our results, it's also a much more fulfilling way to live.

This brings us to the end of the second to last stage of our journey to reach a High-Performing Mind. We've nearly made it! We have one last short segment in front of us. You're already

95% of the way there. Let's find a little extra courage to do what we know we need to do —when we know we need to do it, next.

Two Tools To Perform At Our Best When it Counts:

Tool #1: Use present moment focus to find flow

Tool #2: Use Champion Refocus to get back on track as quickly as possible

Let's Make This Stick

1. List three situations or areas of your life where a present moment focus and being in a flow state would improve your life.

i. _____

ii. _____

iii. _____

2. List three areas, situations, or times in your life when you could practice having a present moment focus.

i. _____

ii. _____

iii. _____

CHAPTER 12

Finding the Courage

Following Your Heart, Taking Chances, and Seizing Opportunities

As I described in Chapter 1, my life path took me from Montreal to Toronto to follow my passion for coaching and playing squash.

Several years after this move, I decided to start an event management company in my spare time. This idea was inspired by a few authors I really connected with at the time and whose books had positively impacted my life. My goal was to bring best-selling authors to Toronto for large-scale public speaking engagements and events.

It was an ambitious plan in an unfamiliar industry, but I was passionate about the idea and determined to make it work.

Having no idea what I was doing, I started by contacting one of these authors through their website to find out their fees for a two-day weekend workshop. Having attended one of their workshops in the past, I knew how helpful it could be, and I hoped to bring that experience to others in Toronto.

The answer to my question was the first dose of cold reality for my event management company idea. I found out that I needed $50,000 upfront just to book the speaker. In fact, the total budget for my first event, which I hoped would attract upwards of 400 people, exceeded my income for an entire year!

It was a jaw-dropping proposition. I had no idea how I would make this work, given I had no investors and hadn't shared my idea with anyone yet.

Unsure what to do, I gave myself a couple of weeks to think it over. I was excited about the opportunity, but worried I wouldn't get enough people to attend and cover my expenses. I wanted others to benefit from this author's work the way I had, but I didn't want to lose any money trying to make this happen!

In the end, I decided to say yes and jumped in with both feet. I just prayed I'd sell enough tickets to cover my costs.

I signed the contract with the author and immediately got to work. I built a website to advertise the workshop and process payments for all the tickets I envisioned selling—I was optimistic, to say the least. I also had to figure out how to get the word out and efficiently advertise the event. I had zero experience with any of this, and you'd think this would have led to many sleepless nights and rampant levels of stress, but somehow, it didn't.

I had no idea how I would pull this crazy idea off, but I really wanted to do it, so I stayed focused on what I was trying to accomplish instead of thinking of all the ways it could fail. I went feverishly to work to make it happen and, more importantly, succeed.

I learned HTML code, which I needed to build the website, placed ads in local newspapers and magazines, printed posters and plastered them around town. I also attended one of the author's workshops in another city to see how it was done. I sourced venues, booked hotel deals for attendees, and secured interviews for the author to promote the event. I also had to find and train a team of thirty volunteers to help me run the whole operation and manage the crowds once it started.

It was a steep learning curve, and I had a rapidly shrinking timeline to complete everything. Regardless, I was determined to make the event a success and, again, not lose any money doing it!

Fast-forward a few months and I had sold enough tickets to cover most of the speaker fee installments, so I didn't have to dip too deeply into my savings.

By the time the big day arrived, I had sold over 400 tickets, which not only covered all my expenses, but made for a decent profit in the end, which was a huge relief!

More importantly, the workshop was a resounding success. The attendees loved it, thanks to the author, who did an outstanding job making it fun and engaging for everyone. I was encouraged enough to do more events with other authors I liked over the next few years.

It was a ton of fun while it lasted, but I eventually wound the company down when an opportunity for a senior management position came along in the hospitality industry. It became increasingly difficult to find the time needed to organize large-scale events, and overall, they weren't profitable or dependable enough to support my family and justify permanently leaving my hospitality career.

Overall, it was an extremely positive experience. I got to meet some famous authors I really admired. I also learned a lot in a short period of time. More importantly, I achieved my goal—thousands of people had attended my events over that period and many expressed how hearing firsthand from some of these fantastic speakers was a life-changing experience for them. Few things could have made me happier.

Tool #1: Go for It When Opportunities Present Themselves and it Feels Right

It all began with one heart-inspired idea. I went for it, even as it led me to make some risky and stress-inducing decisions. My fear of failing motivated me to put in an exceptional amount of time and effort to do everything I could to ensure a successful conclusion. None of this would have happened if I had gotten stopped by negative or fearful thinking.

Following your heart, especially when it involves taking risks and not knowing how you will succeed, can be a daunting prospect. Sometimes, though, we just have to find the courage, take the chance, and go for it. You never know where it will lead. This is our **first tool** for this chapter: Find the courage to **go for it when opportunities present themselves and it feels right.**

Tool #2: Go All In or Fail Spectacularly While Trying

Early in my career competing in sports, I learned that hesitation was a silent killer. Games can move quickly, and decisions and opportunities are often thrust upon us at a rapid rate. As mentioned in Chapter 10, I had many instances when I saw an opportunity but was too scared to make a mistake, and either hesitated—which often resulted in an error of some kind—or decided to play it safe and not take the risk.

Not only did this lead to a conservative style of play in my early years of competing—due to being too focused on the prospect of failing—it also placed limits on my level of success. I didn't take risks often enough and let opportunities go by unless I was confident and sure ahead of time.

Fortunately, my play-it-safe approach diminished over time. I learned that if I didn't take some risks when opportunities came along, I would miss out and fail anyway, so I may as well try. This was a key component in finding greater levels of success as I progressed in the sports I competed in.

Of course, these principles apply outside of sports as well. We benefit from seizing opportunities when they come along; hesitation or waiting too long can mean failure and letting greater levels of success slip by.

I also learned that if I was going to go for something, go for it with 100% effort and everything I had. If I was going to fail, then in the words of Ransom Riggs, I was going to "fail spectacularly" and at least learn something along the way to improve for a future day.

This was the case about ten years ago when my brother and I were sitting around one day and chatting about an idea I had to launch a social networking software application. My concept was to design and develop an app to help connect people through their common interests and hobbies.

I envisioned an app where a person interested in painting, for example, could find other people interested in painting nearby—potentially right around the corner in their own neighborhood. Of course, this app would be able to sort by age, gender, other interests, etc. The hope was to connect people for any activity they could think of, from books to a specific sport, cooking, tequila tasting, playing poker, or board games—the possibilities were endless.

I wanted to help people build friendships and groups world-wide through their common hobbies and activities. It was a bold idea—or so I thought at the time, and this conversation with my brother took place not long after the social networking boom, which saw so many successful software companies surge to success. I thought, *if they could do it, why couldn't I?*

As is commonly the case with family members, they often see things similarly, and my brother John loved the idea. He had been a serial entrepreneur since he finished college and never looked back. He had several successful companies and was a daring risk taker in my opinion. He told me he would be willing to back me financially if I was serious about moving forward with my idea. We would be 50-50 partners in the new venture.

Sure enough, I decided to go for it, and in my spare time, outside of my career in the hospitality industry, I quietly launched my first software company.

Over the next two years, I worked my full-time job in hospitality, helped out around the house with our two young children, and then spent every moment of my free time staying up late and working on building this software company into what I hoped would be a global success—I dream big, I guess…

It was again a steep learning curve, much more so than the event management company ever was, because I was in completely foreign territory. I was designing user interfaces, working with software engineers, and trying to wrap my head around the benefits of different programming languages, the intricacies of digital marketing, and the necessity of advanced tracking analytics. I also studied other successful social networks to determine what elements and concepts we should emulate.

My first big takeaway was that software development was very expensive unless you were doing it yourself. As is often the case in this industry, I was burning through cash at an alarming rate with the goal of getting a finished and usable application to market as soon as possible. This created tremendous pressure to succeed and, unlike my event management company, did lead to many sleepless nights as I worried intensely about wasting my brother's money and the prospect of failing.

Finally, two plus years later, we launched our social networking app with visions of thousands of users flocking to it and it growing into a massive success.

Initial uptake was actually quite good. The software we developed worked reasonably well, despite the large number of bugs we had to work through, and people were able to navigate around and interact with others successfully. We had one big problem however— "churn!" This was an industry term to describe how many people were giving our application a shot and trying it out, but disappointingly, they weren't sticking around.

This churn ended up being a problem that I was never able to solve. I just couldn't get enough people onto our platform quickly enough to sustain growth in each geographical area to get it to succeed. There was just too much distance between users with common interests or not enough local meet-up options for them to find it worthwhile.

I consulted experts, made many changes to the app, tweaked our focus, and changed strategies and direction countless times over the next year, but nothing seemed to work. In the end, we had to finally throw in the towel. It was losing too much money too quickly. It was one colossal failure, and this little app experiment of ours lost more money than I'm comfortable sharing.

On top of that, I had let my brother down. I wasted thousands of hours, which impacted my immediate family, who had to endure my preoccupation with this business venture and my absence during a fair amount of family time. Not a good outcome to say the least.

On a personal level? In short, I had gone "all in" and failed spectacularly. While I learned a huge amount in a variety of new subjects, it was unequivocally a failure of epic proportions.

I had never failed at anything so thoroughly before. I was disappointed to say the least and it did unfortunately create some tensions with John. Thankfully, we eventually resolved things and put it behind us. We always said we'd never let money come between family, and I'm grateful we were able to do this.

Fortunately, my career in the hospitality industry over the years has always been rock solid with many promotions and leadership opportunities. It has remained a backbone of stability, which afforded me the confidence and know-how in many instances to take risks and forge in new directions at various times throughout my life. Besides, just because we failed once, doesn't mean we're doomed to fail again. The past doesn't equal the future.

Tool #3: Find the Courage to Try Again

And this brings us to today, or more accurately, the time of writing. It has been my life-long dream to write a book. From the time I was eighteen years old, I knew I would write a book one day; I just never knew exactly what it would be about.

I always had the general idea that I wanted it to be helpful to others, but it wasn't clear what that would look like for a very long time. I thought about it consistently over the years, a concept in the back of my mind, and the subject matter was constantly changing and evolving as I changed and evolved.

I had to live, fail, figure things out, succeed here and there, and overcome a mountain of challenges before I felt ready. I had to understand what it took to excel, overcome adversity, and find lasting success—for myself and others. More importantly, I had to test and determine what was helpful to others and what was not, deepen my understanding of all this over decades, and fine-tune my message.

Like everyone does when they embark upon an unknown path toward an unseeable destination, I had to endure doubts, fears, naysayers, and challenging periods where it felt like I would never succeed.

But here I am, having written *A High-Performing Mind*, and here you are, having read it. Good thing I never gave up or listened to those doubts for any length of time and resolved to go for it anyway.

Life will always be full of ups and downs and failures and successes. While it's important to know when to move in a new direction, we don't want to quit out of frustration when things don't go well, stop trying when doubts make us question our ability to succeed, or give up prematurely on our dreams. In these moments, if it's important to us, it's in our best interests to find the courage to try again even when succeeding isn't guaranteed.

It can be a frightening experience to move into unfamiliar territory. But, if we can find the courage to take some calculated risks every now and then, go for it when it feels right, or try again after a big failure, it can be the difference between mediocrity and living our best life.

Three Tools To Follow Our Heart, Take Chances, and Seize Opportunities:

Tool #1: Go for it when opportunities present themselves and it feels right

Tool #2: Go All In or Fail Spectacularly While Trying

Tool #3: Find the Courage to Try Again

PART III

– THE VERANDA –

Strengthening the Spirit

CONCLUSION

The End is Just the Beginning of Your New Future

The High-Performing Human Being

Congratulations, you've completed your climb to the top of our hill! You've come a long way, taken every step, and collected all the needed tools to strengthen your mindsets, heart, and spirit and develop your own High-Performing Mind. Let's take this moment to reflect on what you've accomplished.

To start, you are now clear about what you want and have the mental strength, resilience, and discipline to overcome any setbacks and obstacles and to respond constructively in the face of adversity—no matter how difficult.

You understand what it takes to make the most of failures and how to reset after setbacks to still achieve your goals. You see the importance of establishing positive habits that can power you through to anything you set your mind to. And you know that always doing your best enhances how things go in your daily life and immensely increases your chances of achieving your goals over the long term. You are also aware of the value of keeping an open mind—one that is willing to look at its weaknesses for opportunities to improve and have developed the emotional armor to ensure nobody can knock you off course.

If you've reached this point, you're hopefully noticing changes in your mindset and are enjoying some of the benefits.

Simultaneously, you have begun to master your mind. You are focused on the process instead of the outcome to help you achieve your goals. And, you have harnessed the power of your patience, with a little self-restraint thrown in here and there, for good measure. You are more aware of your thinking processes and how to overcome the negative mental spiral that can derail you emotionally and block your success. This also increases your ability to respond positively and constructively during challenging moments.

Most importantly, you have developed the powerful mindset to say YES to fear and to keep going toward the outcomes you're aiming for. When you "hear the fear," you will do something about it—this is not only a constructive response, but it also maximizes your chances of living your optimal life.

By staying open-minded and not latching onto preconceived ideas, you have become a better, more creative problem solver. Finally, you can find flow moments by having the present moment focus and champion refocus to bring your best to the important success defining moments of your life.

Using these tools regularly can help you through adversity and those difficult life-reckoning times. Nobody can promise that life will be easy or all your dreams will come true. But by developing a High-Performing Mind, you can make the most of every card you're dealt.

Developing a High-Performing Mind is an ongoing process, not a destination. There will always be something to work on and toward—even when you're satisfied with how things are going. If you're willing to give your full 100% effort and to continuously make the most of each moment, one day, you'll be able to look back at the extraordinary life you've created.

The End? Imagine

I think the best place to end our journey through *A High-Performing Mind* is back at the beginning. We will do this by revisiting your primary desire from Chapter 1 and Master List of goals from Chapter 6. Only this time, instead of developing them for the first time, you are going to travel five years into the future and imagine what your life might look like then.

Let's try this now. Think about your top few desires and goals. What does your life look like five years from now when you have already achieved them? How do you feel? How did these goals impact the quality of your life? How are you the same or different when you interact with others around you? How are you performing in your daily tasks, activities, and during those key moments in your life that matter most? And most importantly, how would this all feel?

Your future is created in the present. It all begins now by bringing your High-Performing Mind into your daily life and creating the reality you dream of. Only this time, there's nothing that can hold you back.

Keep going!

The 12 Attributes of A High-Performing Mind

The High-Performing Human Being

#1: Intense DESIRE to succeed and the discipline to do something daily to create it.

#2: The expectation it won't be easy and the willingness to give whatever time and effort needed to succeed.

#3: The habit of always doing your best—even if you might fail.

#4: The willingness to improve or change what holds you back.

#5: The resilience to not let other people's negative words or doubts deflate your enthusiasm to succeed.

#6: The ability and openness to learn, adjust, and to keep going after mistakes, setbacks, or failures.

#7: The passion to explore, experiment, improve your skills, and master your craft.

#8: Focused on the process not the outcome.

#9: Focused on positive actions—even when things get negative or bleak.

#10: Say YES to fear, use it, and keep going.

#11: Use present-moment focus to achieve your best performances and maximize your success.

#12: The courage to try again and follow your heart.

STAY IN TOUCH

I hope you enjoyed reading *A High-Performing Mind*. If you did, **leaving a review on Amazon and Goodreads would be greatly appreciated!** It helps others trust that *A High-Performing Mind* is helpful and worth reading.

For Interviews, Keynote Speaking, Coaching, and Consulting opportunities, please reach out to contact@andrewdthompson.com

For more content, articles, and videos on related topics, please visit www.andrewdthompson.com and join my newsletter. It isn't a regular weekly thing, but I do send it out when I feel like I have something worth saying. You can also follow along below on social media.

Follow Andrew on Instagram: andrewthompson9911
Follow Andrew on Threads: andrewthompson9911
Follow Andrew on X/ Twitter: @aandrewthompson
Follow Andrew on YouTube: youtube.com/@andrewdthompson
Follow Andrew on Facebook: facebook.com/people/Andrew-D-Thompson/61565692531103/
Follow Andrew on LinkedIn: linkedin.com/in/athompson99/

ABOUT THE AUTHOR

Andrew D. Thompson has spent a lifetime searching for the best ways to empower people to overcome adversity, strengthen the mind, improve resilience, and consistently bring their best to everything they do so that they can, get better daily results, achieve their goals and find lasting success.

Andrew shares the most powerful habits, mindsets, insights, and mental tools of high-performers from his time and experience as a professional athlete, high-performance coach, hospitality industry executive, and individual who had to overcome some of life's most difficult challenges.

Andrew has been coaching and helping people of all ages and all walks of life, including elite athletes, high performers, and business leaders over the last 25+ years learn how to improve focus, clarity and resilience, get past their setbacks and failures, overcome challenging times, and break through the barriers that block them from improving their circumstances and living more fulfilling lives.

Made in United States
Troutdale, OR
05/17/2025